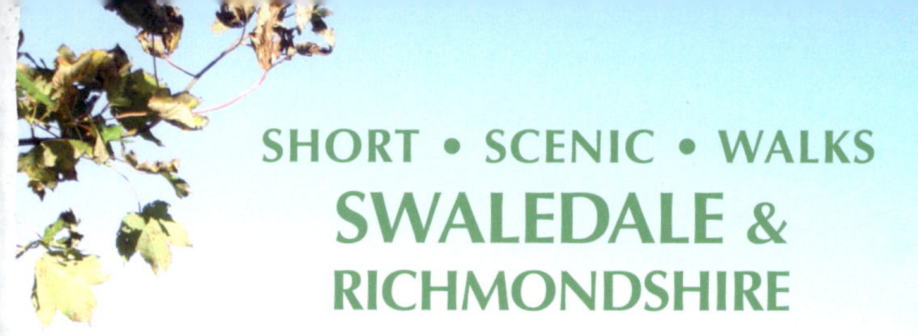

SHORT • SCENIC • WALKS
SWALEDALE & RICHMONDSHIRE

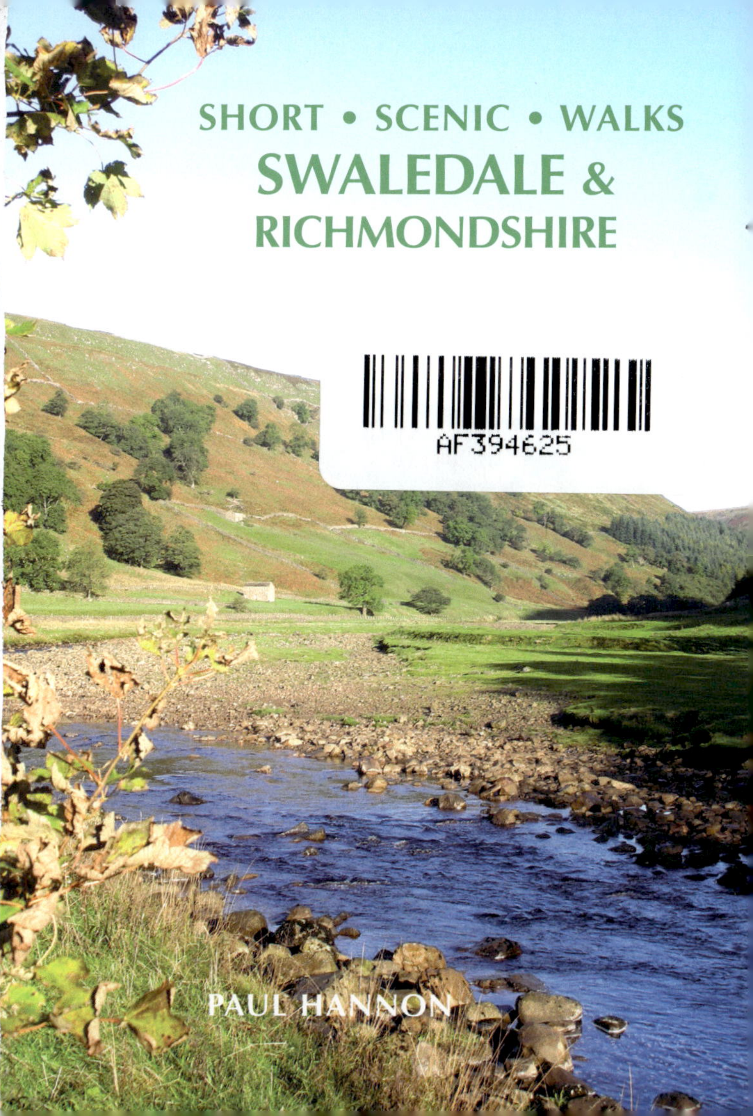

PAUL HANNON

HILLSIDE PUBLICATIONS

38 Westburn Avenue, Keighley, West Yorkshire BD22 6AW

First Published 2026   © Paul Hannon 2026

ISBN 978 1 907626 36 4

Sketch maps based on OS 1947 1-inch maps

Cover illustrations: The Swale above Gunnerside; Muker
Back cover: Old Gang Smelt Mill; Page 1: The Swale near Muker
(Paul Hannon/Yorkshire Photo Library)

Printed in China on behalf of Latitude Press

HILLSIDE GUIDES... cover much of Northern England

- 60 Classic Yorkshire Dales Walks (hardback omnibus edition)
- 50 Yorkshire Walks For All (short strolls from 2 to 3 miles)
- Mountains of the Yorkshire Dales (25 hillwalks to all 31 peaks)
- Journey of the Wharfe (photographic hardback)

Short Scenic Walks • Swaledale & Richmondshire • Wensleydale
- Three Peaks & Malham • Haworth & Aire Valley • Wharfedale & Ilkley
- Ribble Valley & Bowland • Arnside & Lunesdale • North York Moors
- Harrogate & Nidderdale • Teesdale & Weardale • South Pennines
- Ambleside & South Lakeland • Pendle & Lancashire Moors

Walking in Yorkshire
- Aire Valley & Bronte Country
- Harrogate & Ilkley
- Nidderdale & Ripon
- Wharfedale & Malham
- North York Moors South & West
- Yorkshire Wolds
- South Yorkshire
- Calderdale & South Pennines
- Countryside around Leeds
- Three Peaks & Howgill Fells
- Wensleydale & Swaledale
- North York Moors North & East
- Richmondshire & Hambleton
- Howardian Hills & Vale of York

Long Distance Walks • Dales Way • Coast to Coast Walk

Kisdon Force, Keld

At Muker

CONTENTS

INTRODUCTION

Swaledale is a very well-defined valley, from the River Swale's beginnings in the shadow of the wild Pennines to its departure from the National Park near Richmond. Remoteness from centres of population has helped it remain relatively unchanged: throughout its length the dale remains steep-sided and loses little grandeur. The only sizeable tributary is Arkle Beck, which flows through Arkengarthdale to Reeth, and shares the characteristics of its parent valley. Swaledale's collection of idyllic villages is one of its finest assets: the upper dale settlements of Keld, Thwaite, Muker and Gunnerside are characterful huddles of stone cottages, nestled amid a patchwork of pastures filled with archetypal field barns.

Swaledale's varied walking leads from flower-filled meadows to heather moors, and encounters beautiful waterfalls and idyllic riverbank. An intense concentration of 19th century lead mining remains touch almost every corner of the dale, from the mines on the moors down through the gills with their smelt mills to the tiny villages of miners' cottages. England's highest pub sits amid old coal mines at lonely Tan Hill, while Swaledale's most impressive single historical feature is the imposing Norman castle above the river at Richmond. This magnificent gateway to the valley is one of the finest little towns in the land, its medieval charm and character being a perfect match for the dale it guards. Beyond this archetypal Dales valley is a wealth of peaceful, attractive settlements that add their own charm to this part of Richmondshire.

These 30 walks comprise diverse strolls leading to every type of landscape, with half a dozen briefly crossing Open Access land: of these only a couple involve grouse moors, which can be closed on a limited number of days (not normally Sundays) and dogs are permitted only on rights of way: details from Natural England and information centres. Whilst the route description should be sufficient to guide you around, a good map is recommended for greater information and interest: Ordnance Survey Explorer map OL30 covers 24 of the walks, with the others served by Explorer 304.

Information
•Yorkshire Dales National Park (www.yorkshiredales.org.uk)
Yoredale, Bainbridge, Leyburn DL8 3EL
•Market Hall **Richmond** DL10 4QL • 01748-826468
•Hudson House **Reeth** Richmond DL11 6SZ • 01748-884059

SWALEDALE & RICHMONDSHIRE
30 Short Scenic Walks

3³⁄4 miles from Tan Hill

Moorland paths amid the bleak surrounds of Britain's highest pub

Start *Tan Hill Inn (NY 897066; DL11 6ED), roadside parking*
Map *OS Explorer OL30, Yorkshire Dales, North/Central (or OL19)*

At 1725ft/526m the Tan Hill Inn is renowned as Britain's highest pub. Its wild moorland setting is pitted with coal mines that served lead smelting mills in Swaledale and Arkengarthdale. Minor roads arrive at this meeting place of drovers' and packhorse ways from Keld via Stonesdale, Reeth via Arkengarthdale and Stainmore via Barras: Pennine Wayfarers view the hostelry as a veritable oasis. This enforced isolation has seen less resilient landlords survive only one harsh winter before accepting defeat. Each May a long-established sheep show is a major event. The place has also found its way into the news at regular intervals, notably a 1980s double glazing TV advertisement with ensuing planning problems. and a wrangle over geographical identity that featured a temporary transfer to Durham from its rightful county.

From the pub cross the road and head away on the broad stony track of the Pennine Way, this first section being an old mine track. Rising very slightly it affords big views: to the right is Nine Standards Rigg, while to the left, above you, is sprawling Rogan's Seat. When the track bends left take the Pennine Way right, becoming immediately grassier to run a splendid, largely level course for some time. The slightest of declines leads to crossing the beginnings of a small gill: the path drops a little right, down to a junction with an old track doubling sharply back right. You keep left for a good level section, soon dropping a more sustained course to the right down Stonesdale Moor. In front over the head of Swaledale are the broad shoulders of Great Shunner Fell, with Lovely Seat to its left and High Seat's Mallerstang ridge to the right.

When the Pennine Way prepares to drop into the adjacent sizeable ravine of Lad Gill, don't descend to the simple footbridge but turn right on a broad, grassy quad track. This drops between reeds to soon join the Keld-Tan Hill moorland road below, just above a stone-arched bridge on Lad Gill. Turn right for half a mile's very gentle rise along the road, making use of some decent verges. As the road starts to swing right to climb steeply by another side gill, leave it and drop left on a soft track through reeds to reach crumbling sheepfolds alongside Stonesdale Beck. The track crosses at a ford, but all you need do is turn upstream the few yards to a slab footbridge just beneath a confluence with modest Thomas Gill. Again don't cross, but trace a thin and intermittently built path upstream, quickly leaving it to return closer opposite another stone fold on the bank above a little waterfall. Just beyond is a tiny outcrop projecting above a confluence, and here leave the gill as the path turns right to rise by Tan Gill. This neat grassy path climbs away to ultimately regain the road, and the pub appears just five easy minutes distant.

Tan Hill Inn

3¾ miles from Hoggarths

A fine circuit of a lonely dalehead valley

*Start Hoggarths (NY 870013; DL11 6LT),
Riverside parking area on B6270
at High Bridge, east of farm
Map OS Explorer OL30, Yorkshire
Dales, North/Central (or OL19)*

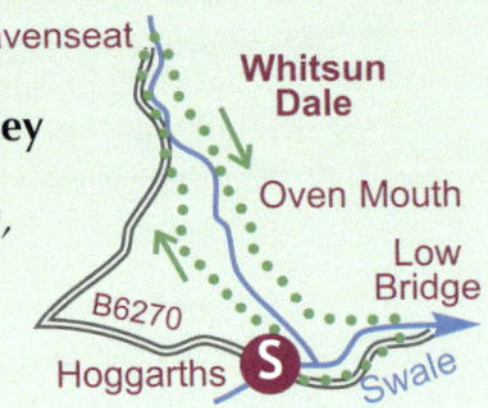

First of all take time to appreciate the delectable River Swale here, formed just a stone's throw to the west by the meeting of Birkdale Beck and Great Sleddale Beck. From a slender wall-stile directly opposite the parking area, head across the field, bearing right up to a wall-stile by a solitary tree. Ascend the next field with the wall, passing a fine barn to a stile at the top. A thin trod heads away with the wall on your right, and when the wall drops away you meet a grassy track. Advance along this to a wall-stile ahead. A path now rises left past an island barn to a gap-stile above. Initially pathless, bear right to meet an improving quad track dropping right to cross a streamlet beneath a curved wall.

Rising towards a barn, a thin trod bears off left up to a gap-stile just ahead. A little path runs right with the wall, past a barn where Ravenseat appears ahead. The path now runs more directly to meet the wall again at a corner ladder-stile. It resumes with the

wall to quickly join the moorland road to Ravenseat. Turn right to its demise at the farm, en route crossing a cattle-grid off the moor where the Coast to Coast Walk comes in. In an oasis of green fields in a moorland hollow, Ravenseat is a typical upland sheep farm that gained national prominence thanks to TV exposure. Refreshments are often available.

Entering the farm environs bear right, crossing Whitsundale Beck on a neat arched bridge and then a second stream to rise towards a house. Here take a gap-stile on the right, heading away to another as a broad path runs briefly with Whitsundale Beck. Past an old square sheepfold and through a gate above an attractive waterfall, the path rises away to a barn. A largely level course now runs past further barns and gateways amid rough pastures: path improvements for the C-C have seen several flagged sections installed. After gazing into the splendid wooded gorge of How Edge Scars, level pastures with a wall for company precede emergence through a last gate into a dramatic scene above Oven Mouth. This highlight of Whitsun Dale features colourful, craggy slopes plunging to an ox-bow on the beck. The wall now fades as you contour grandly across open country, with views over to an archetypal Dales landscape of scattered barns amid the fields.

Soon passing along the bottom side of a large crumbling, sloping enclosure, a very gentle descent runs across to Smithy Holme, whose barns now form a desirable residence. Its access road runs left to a gate off the open moor, and down past another farm conversion to drop past a limekiln to stone-arched Low Bridge on the Swale. Joining the B6270, turn right for the final stage, rising above the river with a prospect of the Whitsundale Beck confluence before dropping again, passing a waterfall on the Swale to return to High Bridge.

The Swale at Hoggarths

Opposite: at Ravenseat

4³⁄4 miles from Keld

Beautiful moments on and around the youthful Swale

Start Village centre (NY 892011; DL11 6DZ), car park *Map* OS Explorer OL30, Yorkshire Dales, North/Central (or OL19)

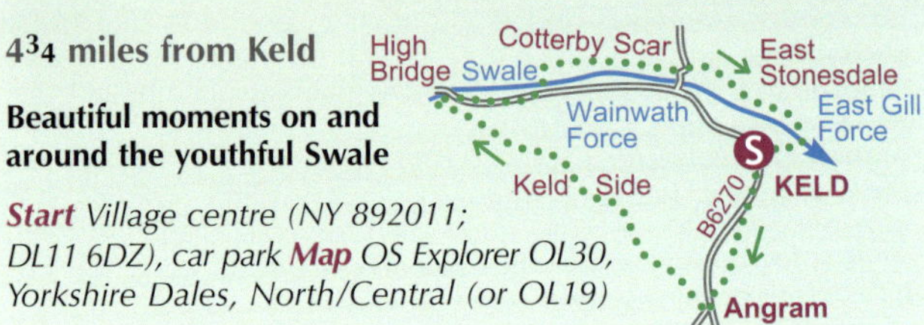

For a note on Keld see page 12. From the square climb to the main road and go left out of the village for a few minutes. 120 yards after a bridleway drops left, take a stile on the left and bear right to another. An intermittent path maintains this course through fields with regular stiles. At one shortly after a fine barn, with no stile visible, cross to a footbridge on Ay Gill right of trees. Head away to a bridle-gate, then on to a stile and past a barn to briefly follow a track to a stile ahead. At the next stile just left of a gate by a second successive barn, slant right up a grass track to a gate onto the road just left of a house in the hamlet of Angram. Go briefly left to the phonebox and take a side road right. Leave at once by a gate on the right, and a sunken way doubles back up the field. Just beyond a limekiln, pass through a gate to be briefly enclosed. Emerging, head away through reeds to meet a grassy quad track on the brow ahead. Go briefly left to soon bear right to a gate in a wall just ahead, meeting another such track leading to it. A thin trod follows a wall away, and as it drops away contour on to a wall-stile ahead.

Advance through a minor dip to a stile on the brow. Now advance briefly to meet a grassy quad track, going left with it above the trough of Ay Gill. A path forms at an old wall junction, where bear right on a grassy way. Keep right to angle around and gently down into Ay Gill, soon reaching a stile in the wall onto the base of a heather bank. A thin path runs left to a stile at the end on Keld Side. Sweeping views to the Swale's high watershed feature High Seat and Nine Standards Rigg. An improving little path heads away, soon revealing the limestone of Cotterby Scar way over to the right. Dropping very gently, keep left above denser reeds to a stile in a descending wall. The path runs on to drop to a shooters' track just beyond a footbridge on Blackburn Beck.

A scrappy cairn almost opposite indicates the onward path. Rising slightly, it soon swings right, and down to a ladder-stile beneath a barn. Two further such stiles feature on this slant, with High Bridge and the Swale appearing below. Dropping onto a firm riverside track, go briefly right to the B6270 at High Bridge. Turn right, soon climbing away before dropping back to cross stone-arched Low Bridge. *Note that to enjoy the scar, river and falls you would need to remain on the road from here.* A stony track climbs past a limekiln, but leave at the first trees on an inviting path right above an old wall to commence a level stroll above the length of unseen Cotterby Scar: there are however, glimpses of the river.

From a gate at the end a grass track slants gently down with a wall, with Wainwath Force largely obscured by trees below. Remain on the field top to a gate onto a steep road, crossing to a driveway opposite. Approaching Stonesdale Beck, Currack Force is just off-route before the bridge, with a nice waterfall immediately below the bridge itself. A little pull precedes a largely level stroll to East Stonesdale Farm. A track turns down between buildings through a gate to drop steeply to a path junction above East Gill Force, a delectable spot. Take the path down the near side of the waterfall to a footbridge on the Swale. The path climbs right, and keep right to run enclosed back into Keld. Catrake Force can be visited on a courtesy path at Rukins Farm in the square.

East Gill Force

3^{1}2 miles from Keld

The Swale Gorge hides a dramatic ravine that this walk eagerly explores

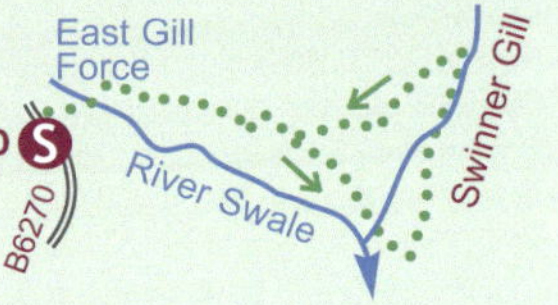

Start *Village centre (NY 892011; DL11 6DZ), car park*
Map *OS Explorer OL30, Yorkshire Dales, North/Central*

Keld is the first outpost of any size in Swaledale, an idyllic spot where the Pennine Way and Coast to Coast Walk cross paths. Most of this Norse settlement is set around a tiny square below the main road. The Institute houses a Countryside & Heritage Centre, and the old school a Living Heritage Museum. A fine sundial adorns a United Reformed Church of 1861, with WCs alongside. A Great War memorial recalls four men who never returned to their village. The former shooting lodge then youth hostel of Keld Lodge has a public bar, with refreshments also available at Rukins Park Lodge campsite and at a café up on the through road.

Leave the bottom right corner of the square by a broad, walled path past a barn. Quickly reaching a fork, take the left branch steeply down to a footbridge on the River Swale. Across, a path curves up above delightful East Gill Force (see page 11) to the Pennine Way and Coast to Coast junction. Turn right over a stone-arched bridge and a broad, stony track climbs away, levelling out above a steep, fenced scree slope high above the Swale Gorge. The way soon opens out to swing round past a barn beneath Beldi Hill's lead mining remains to quickly reach a fork. You will return by the left branch, so for now take the stony track slanting right, down into trees to wind all the way down to a gate at the bottom in front of a footbridge and ford on Swinner Gill. On your left stand the remains of Beldi Hill smelt mill, with a waterfall behind.

Across, the track slants up a little bank behind into open terrain. Leave within a couple of minutes at the start of a fenced, part-wooded, springtime bluebell-draped enclosure just up to the left. From the fence corner a grassy path ascends outside the fence, soon swinging left to slant more steadily across into bracken. This soon eases to reveal the colourful enclave of Swinner Gill you are about to penetrate. It runs delightfully on into the gill, enjoying waterfalls below and gleaming scars above, whilst taking a little care with your footing. Over a fence-stile above another waterfall, you quickly slant in to join the stream itself above yet another waterfall. Amid rugged surrounds water flows from a stone level. Cross here on well-placed stones to the continuing path slanting right up the other side. Ignore an early left fork and continue climbing above the stream's craggy walls, rising through a modest rocky band. A super level walk ensues to meet a broader path just short of a stone-arched bridge on Swinner Gill. Just across the gill at the foot of the side valley of East Grain stand the remains of a lead-smelting mill, below which is a waterfall and arched level.

Double back left across a small spoilheap to slant delightfully up across this heathery flank. The path runs on through a few rocks to a gate in a wall. The grassy way swings right to run through bracken down past an old mine building and beneath substantial spoil to drop down alongside ruinous Crackpot Hall. This former farmhouse was abandoned long ago as a result of mining subsidence: its view down the Swale Gorge remains spectacular. The way swings right here to soon merge with your outward route to retrace steps to Keld.

Smelt mill, Swinner Gill

4 miles from Keld

Even by Upper Swaledale standards this is an awesome, beautiful walk

Start *Village centre (NY 892011; DL11 6DZ), car park*
Map *OS Explorer OL30, Yorkshire Dales, North/Central*

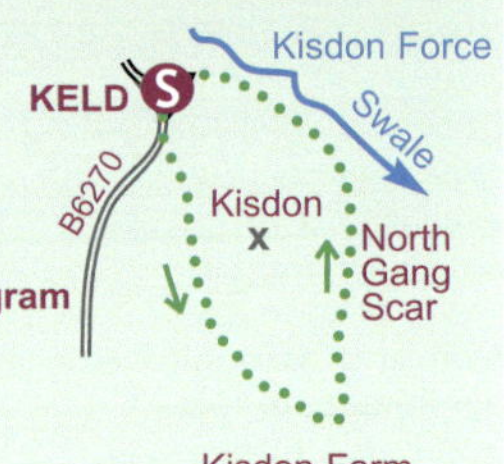

For a note on Keld see page 12. Leave the square by the road rising left to the main road, and turn left along it a short way until a walled, stony access road drops left by a barn. This old way will lead unerringly over the hill to Muker. It is the first and most impressive section of a former 'corpse road' which ran all the way down the valley to Grinton. For the deceased of the Keld area it was only the start of a long trip for burial prior to Muker acquiring its own consecrated ground. Crossing a streamlet by ford and slab footbridge it climbs steeply away, but after a gate it rises more gently across open pasture. Big views of the mountains around the dalehead stretch from Lovely Seat to Great Shunner Fell, High Seat and Nine Standards Rigg. Opposite is the hamlet of Angram.

Easing out further, the track runs beneath an isolated house, and when it swings left to serve it, your onward way transforms into a superb green way to a gate in a wall ahead. A long pasture is crossed, still rising ever gently until approaching Hooker Mill Scar, it swings left up to a gate in the parallel wall. Rising to another gate, it runs on between old walls by mining debris. Through a further gateway it rises very gently along the edge of moorland. Kisdon's unfrequented summit stands at 1637ft/499m a good half-mile over to the left. Arrival at a gate in a wall ahead finally marks the summit of the walk at around 1607ft/490m. By now the first views ahead have appeared, with sombre moors across the Swale Gorge leading around to Rogan's Seat.

The way drops away with a wall on the left, soon revealing Swinner Gill, Arn Gill and Ivelet scars opposite, and more of the main valley. The way soon abandons the true path which drops to a corner then turns right, short-cutting it to slant down to become briefly enclosed at the far corner. Emerging, continue down the wallside to meet the Pennine Way coming in from the right. Here bear left on a little path the short way to meet a track just above a barn conversion. Go left up this green way towards a corner. Ignoring a continuing track rising left, a path rises with the wall on your right to a small corner gate. Pass through to commence a classic walk along the undulating terrace of North Gang Scar, through gateways and stiles and occasional rashes of stones. This traverses Kisdon's flank with spectacular views over the finest section of the Swale backed by Swinner Gill under Rogan's Seat.

Eventually reaching Rukin Wood, the path follows the slope round to the left above it for a sustained spell. Reaching a fork at a gap in the accompanying wall at the wood-end, pass through to slant down to a junction with a broader path. Go left to quickly arrive beneath tall cliffs, where consider a short detour to view Kisdon Force (see page 3). A sign sends a branch right beneath further crags including a detached pinnacle, winding down to a small clearing on a knoll above the Swale. Bearing right, it quickly reaches a junction overlooking the top of the unseen falls: a rough branch drops to rock slabs atop the falls. The onward path traverses further (with a good view of the falls) to a more appealing path doubling back down to a falls-side vantage point. Back on the main path, it quickly becomes enclosed to soon re-enter Keld.

Looking down on the Swale from North Gang Scar

4¹4 miles from Thwaite

**Moorland and meadows on the
flanks of an endearing hill**

Start *Village centre (SD 892981; DL11 6DR),
roadside parking below Buttertubs junction*
Map *OS Explorer OL30,
Yorkshire Dales, North/Central*

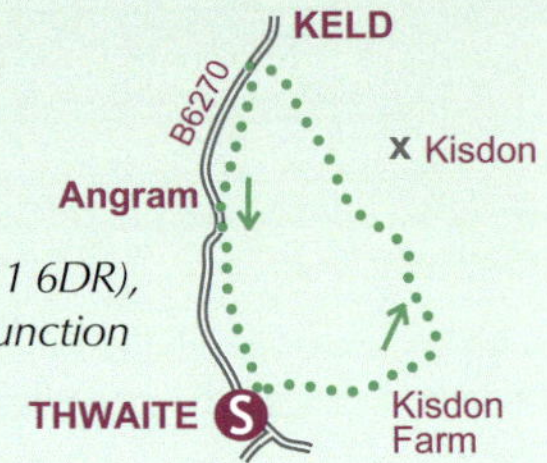

Thwaite is a tiny village that was home to the Kearton brothers, pioneers in nature photography: the popular Kearton Country Hotel offers refreshments. Turn along the short lane in front of the Kearton, and at the end a Pennine Way sign points the way through a short enclosed path by a house just right of a farmyard. Through a gate, a couple of stiles lead into a field where the path forks. Go left on the Pennine Way, across to a gate and on to a farm bridge on Skeb Skeugh. Bear right up the steep field, merging with a wall to rise to a corner stile. A super path slants up through open country to a wall corner. This stage enjoys sweeping views back over the village to Lovely Seat and Great Shunner Fell.

Head on with the wall to a dramatically sited barn with a glimpse of Muker, then up to a stile and on with a wall on your left. This curves round into a broad recess, on through a small gate to swing right with the wall to the rear of Kisdon Farm. Through a gate at the end onto the drive, instead take a gate on the left where a walled green way rises past an old limekiln. Quickly opening out the PW turns right: your way is an ascending wallside way left. Becoming briefly enclosed it emerges into a higher pasture, to slant across to a wall opposite. Rise left with it to a gate, at 1607ft/490m the walk's high point. The splendid grass track heads away, gently declining across moorland. Through a gate it runs between old walls and past mining debris to another, then on to one in the next parallel wall. Ahead are the high fells encircling the dalehead.

The way now bears right across a long pasture, with an isolated house ahead. Pass through a gate at the end, just beyond which its access track comes in. Advance on well below the house, as the now stony track slants more steeply down, becoming fully enclosed for the final section to a streamlet, with ford and slab footbridge. Just up the other side it meets the valley road, where go left 120 yards to a stile. Over it bear right to another, and maintain this course through meadows with regular stiles. At one shortly after a fine barn, with no stile visible, cross to a footbridge right of trees. Head away to a bridle-gate, then on to a stile and past a barn to briefly follow a track to a corner stile ahead. Beyond two more stiles, bear left across a rolling field to a corner stile, then on to a barn on a brow beneath the hamlet of Angram. Dropping gently away with a wall, the path swings right to a stile onto the road.

Go briefly left to a gate/stile on the left, and slant gently away to a stile in an outer wall corner behind a barn. A little path maintains the slant down to bridge a tree-lined streamlet. Through a stile just beyond, follow the left-hand wall away through reedy pastures. The wall ends at a stile by a barn, where drop along a pleasant spur to a pair of barns with a stile in between. A moist corner is negotiated on stone flags, close by tree-lined Skeb Skeugh. The part-flagged path runs to a corner stile with another just beyond, then along a longer meadow to a stile at the end. The path bears briefly left to another corner stile, where advance on through a gap by gates into a concrete yard. Pass left of modern barns to a small gate onto your outward route on the village edge.

The return path along the Corpse Road

3^{1}2 miles from Muker

A simple walk offering good views from low slopes, and linking two lovely tiny villages

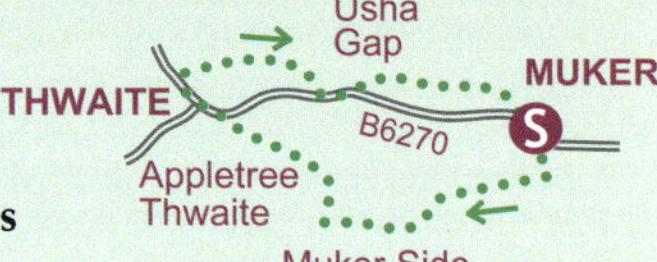

Start Village centre (SD 909978; DL11 6QG), car park
Map OS Explorer OL30, Yorkshire Dales, North/Central

Muker is Swaledale's most picturesque village: a splendid grouping of buildings rising above Straw Beck include the Farmers Arms, shop/tearoom and WC. Though first built in 1580, St Mary's church dates largely from 1890. Other buildings are the Literary Institute of 1868 with a Historical Muker exhibition, and the Public Hall of 1922 behind it. The old school is a craft shop and gallery, and the village pound (for stray livestock) stands by the car park. Muker is home to the Swaledale Agricultural Show in September. Cross the bridge at the east end of the village, and leave the road immediately after the car park by a walled track rising right. This is known as the Occupation Road (farmers' access to the various fields), and beyond some barns it doubles back to commence a sustained slant up towards Muker Side. Increasingly magnificent views look across the valley to Kisdon, while beyond Muker is the Swale Gorge backed by Rogan's Seat.

Ultimately the way swings left to rise to a T-junction of walled tracks at Three Loaning (lane) End. Go right for a near-level stride along Muker Side, a super section with outstanding views over the upper dale, in particular across to Kisdon, while Great Shunner Fell impresses straight ahead. Just beyond crossing a stone-arched bridge on a grassy ravine, turn right down a walled, grassy way as far as a tiny barn on a bend. Here leave by a gate on the left, crossing a field-bottom to become briefly enclosed again before a continuing track passes above Appletree Thwaite. Merging with its drive at a gate at the end, follow it down through a further gate then down a larger field to find a stile just to the right in the bottom corner. This gives a tiny short-cut over a footbridge on Cliff Beck in a little ravine. The track is rejoined just beyond to run out onto the road, with Thwaite soon entered just along to the left beyond the Hawes junction. For a note on Thwaite see Walk 6.

Turn along the short lane in front of Kearton Country Hotel (with teashop), and at the end a Pennine Way sign points you through a ginnel by a house just right of a farmyard: a couple of stiles lead into a field. Here the Way strikes left, but you continue with Thwaite Beck to a wall-stile ahead. As the beck swings away, a thin path keeps straight ahead across three further fields to reach a stone-arched footbridge on a smaller beck, Skeb Skeugh, coming in from the left. Through a stile behind it head away with a wall to a stile at the end, then on past a barn to a stile from where an enclosed beckside path joins the valley road at Usha Gap Bridge. Go briefly left to the farm and up the main drive to the house. Go right through the yard to a gate into a camping field, then bear left to find a stile near the far end. A string of obvious stiles now leads a faint path across the field-bottoms to Muker, waiting ahead: the latter stages are flagged. On entering the village, a little path on the right drops down to emerge alongside the pub (see page 3).

Muker and Kisdon from the Occupation Road

4¾ miles from Muker

A lofty promenade high above the riverbank by which you return

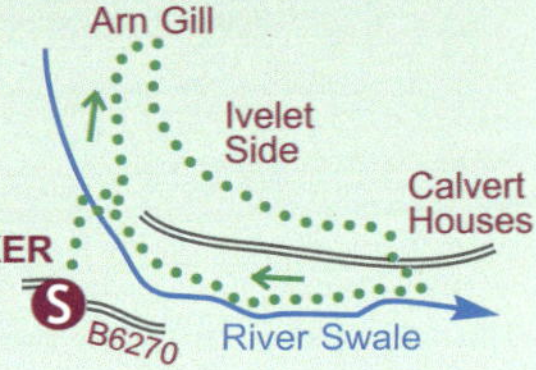

Start *Village centre*
(SD 909978; DL11 6QG), car park
Map *OS Explorer OL30,*
Yorkshire Dales, North/Central
Access *Open Access, see page 4 (no grouse shooting issues)*

For a note on Muker see page 18. Leave by a minor road slanting up behind the Literary Institute at a slender, sloping green. Pass right of an 'island' house and cross to a tiny lane right of the former Post office: a gate/stile into a field reveal the Swale Gorge ahead. Initially a track, by the next gate/stile it becomes a stone-flagged path across six meadows linked by stiles to gain the river. Turn right to a stile to trace the Swale briefly down to Ramps Holme Bridge, a fine viewpoint looking up the valley (see page 1). Across, ascend a stepped path, ignoring an early right branch. The steps then swing left, quickly levelling to run briefly on to a stony track.

Double back right up this, soon levelling before a gentler rise. Making use of Open Access, an inviting grassy way soon doubles back left up through Ivelet Wood. This old miners' path rakes gently up the flank to emerge with big views over the Swale across to Kisdon. Before long it curves round to approach the sidestream of Arn Gill alongside a large spoilheap at a lead mine: across is a stone hut. Without crossing take a slim trod climbing right, shadowing the gill's near side to an arched level with a thin trod above. Double back right on this, rising gently to open out high above the dale floor. Remaining thin but obvious, it soon levels out as the modest escarpment of Ivelet Boards forms above. A moderately airy section awaits, and in slippery conditions an option would be to rise to easier ground above the scar.

Advance on above a minor landslip to approach scattered trees, where pass through modest scree slopes to ease out on Ivelet

Side. Above further minor scars you look down on the village backed by Great Shunner Fell. A scant wall survives alongside, and as this drops away, bear left from the fading edge: an improving way contours round grass slopes to approach the more substantial Kisdon Scar. The fading path rises steadily beneath it and above an old walled quarry to a brow above the quarry end. The grassy track now drops gently down, fading above a large dark, limestone fissure. Just beyond, at a slight dip, bear right to drop to the road between low scars above the hamlet of Calvert Houses. Turn down its short access road into the yard, and take a stile on the left.

Head away past a barn to a corner stile, and from one just a few yards further, slant left down the field to a gate in a fence below. A faint track slants down the next field with the river just below. As it fades drop to a small gate to pick up the valley path. Don't pass through, but follow the path right to join the river and head upstream amid grand scenery. A wooded bank divides a large then a smaller meadow: an early fence-stile on the left then sends a path by the river to a ford at the end. Ignore this and take a facing wall-stile to leave the river, crossing several stiles in parallel walls. The first field features a short branch path to Great Rampsholme cowhouse. Passing Ramps Holme Farm you reach a stile by a barn, and a path runs on with a wall to rejoin the outward route. Drop down to re-cross Ramps Holme Bridge and retrace steps to Muker.

Kisdon from Arn Gill

3³4 miles from Gunnerside

Archetypal meadows lead to Swaledale's finest bridge

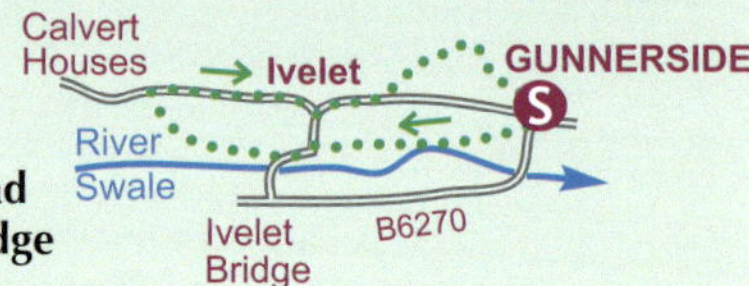

Start Village centre (SD 950982; DL11 6LD), parking by bridge
Map OS Explorer OL30, Yorkshire Dales, North/Central

For a note on Gunnerside see page 26. From the bridge, depart along the lane to the right of the up-dale road, identified by a tiny floral green at the start. The lane soon ends at the school, and a gate to its right leads between modern housing to a stile into a field. A little path heads across several meadows punctuated by a string of stiles (and one gate) to arrive above a bend of the Swale at Marble Scar. Don't take the stile towards the river, but go right up the fenceside to one above the wooded bank. Initially enclosed, it quickly resumes as before, on a largely level course through a longer series of stiles all the way to wooded Shore Gill. Drop to cross the footbridge, and up the other side to emerge into the tiny hamlet of Ivelet. As you enter note a 1761 datestone.

Turn down the road to the river, running upstream with it to Ivelet Bridge. This beautiful old high-arched structure is without doubt the finest crossing of the Swale: at its near side is a stone slab on which coffins were rested in the days when the dead of the upper dale had to be carried all the way down-dale to Grinton church. Don't cross, but take a small gate in front to accompany the Swale upstream just one field's-length. After that the thin path bears right to a small gate at the corner. Instead of returning to the river slant steeply right, a grass track forming to rise to a gate in the fence above. Slant left above it to a stile in the top wall near the left corner. The hamlet of Calvert Houses could be accessed by another stile just to the left, but you simply ascend the fieldside to a small gate at the top. Now rise more steeply left to another in front of cottages. This puts you onto Calvert Houses' access road, a few strides up which it joins another minor road.

Turn right for a delightful, traffic-free stroll along the base of grassy moor, enjoying grand views from this shelf high above the dale. Further on it drops amid lush verges to a junction on a brow behind Gunnerside Lodge. Go left, dropping to bridge Shore Gill and climbing away past Shoregill Head. After a short level spell beneath open moor, it soon starts to drop gently at Dyke Heads. Here take a broad shooters' track forking left on an appreciable climb. At a large cairn it prepares to climb more steeply left: here take a thin path down initially reedy pasture on the right. Lower down the terrain improves, and a grassy continuation approaches a fence enclosing Gunnerside Gill's wooded lower reach to reveal the roofs of Gunnerside. Go right with the fence until it turns away, then continue straight down to a small gate in the bottom corner to drop back down into the village.

Ivelet Bridge

$3^{1}4$ miles from Gunnerside

A fascinating, colourful side valley with lead mining remains

Start *Village centre (SD 950982; DL11 6LD), parking by bridge*
Map *OS Explorer OL30, Yorkshire Dales, North/Central*

For a note on Gunnerside see page 26. Leave the bridge by a driveway on the pub side, following Gunnerside Beck upstream. Having been deflected around the grounds of Gunnarside Hall, small pastures lead the path along open surrounds until a stile puts you into a wooded bank of the beck. A clearer path now runs by the beck and a few boulders, on through a small gate and into denser woodland. A good path enjoys a sustained stroll through this long sliver of woodland from where you rise above the beck. This early part of the walk, through beautiful woodland contrasts with the wilder scenes which will soon dominate.

The wood is left in impressive surrounds as you near Gunnerside Beck again, dropping to a plank bridge and stile out of the trees into an open strath. An adjacent stile sends you along a wallside and through two further wall-stiles to reach the remains of a crushing mill. A long row of bunkers behind was for storing lead ore. Just past the ruins along this lawn-like pasture, a small fence-gate sends the path right, rising to run along a wallside to emerge above a steep bank of the beck opposite a substantial ruin. This is a former mine 'shop', an office of the Sir Francis Mine.

Here leave the valley floor at a stile in the adjacent wall. An inviting, broad green path slants up through bracken, keeping eyes peeled for an early crossroads with a lesser path beneath a rash of stones (before the first wall corner is reached). Turn right on this, slanting up through bracken and becoming fainter to approach a descending wall. Directly behind a low ruin, a narrow wall-stile sends an intermittent trod across two field tops, emerging via a stile at the far corner into open pasture. Continue straight on a thin path with a short embanked section to pass a tiny section of wall (an old sheep shelter). At a wall beyond, keep well above it to rise gently onto a super green track. Bear right on it, becoming part enclosed to soon reach the isolated house at Winterings beneath Low Scar. Bear round to the left to meet the driveway at the front. Easiest option follows the drive out and all the way down to Gunnerside, but a nicer field-path awaits.

Immediately on your right, cross a fence-stile into a paddock. Cross to a wall-stile to commence a splendid, undulating crossing of fields linked by stiles. At the end you approach three buildings, the middle one a barn. Pass right of the left-hand cottage of Pot Ing and on to a gate just beyond, where its grassy drive drops away in sunken fashion. Through a gate and across a streamlet, it rises onto a surfaced road. Turn right past High Bents and Low Bents to commence a steep spiral down towards Gunnerside, which now appears below. Two grassy short-cuts on the right eschew sharp zigzags, and the road's final slant left can be cut part way down by bearing right down a grassy way. At the bottom double back a few yards to reach a gate between houses onto a small green in the village. This final stage affords a classic bird's-eye view over the rooftops.

Gunnerside Beck, Gunnerside Gill

4½ miles from Gunnerside

A simple stroll never far from the River Swale

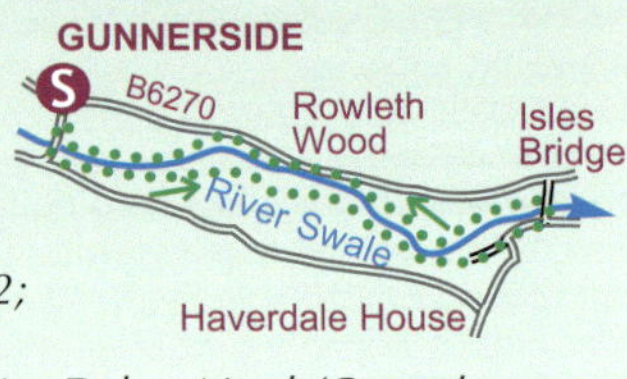

Start *Village centre (SD 950982; DL11 6LD), parking by bridge*
Map *OS Explorer OL30, Yorkshire Dales, North/Central*

Gunnerside, like most of its neighbours, had its heyday in lead mining times. It was founded by the Norsemen, and it seems Gunnar was a Viking chieftain. There is the Kings Head pub, a tearoom and WC. The Literary Institute of 1877 serves as village hall, and there is a Wesleyan Methodist Chapel of 1806. The village stands astride its own beck, which apart from a level quarter-mile from here to the Swale, spends its time tumbling down the deep gill immediately above the village. Take the Muker road out of the village, shadowing Gunnerside Beck to its confluence with the Swale at Gunnerside New Bridge.

Across, leave rapidly, before the Crackpot junction by a short path on the left, quickly rising to a small gate, then up onto a hard track just above. This is Dubbing Garth Lane, which leads unfailingly left down-dale. After a drop to river level it settles down to a long stride enclosed by walls, a once delectable grassy way now entirely firm underfoot. A relatively brief spell by the river midway precedes running through trees below Dubbing Garth and along to Haverdale House. Becoming surfaced it quickly reaches a junction with a through road at the Old Parsonage. Turn left and keep left to soon reach the three arches of Isles Bridge. Attractive cottages occupy the far bank.

Cross the bridge and use a stile on the left to commence the return, briefly by the wide river's stony bank. Two early crossings of water channels precede a brief open section, quickly crossing a slab bridge on a trickle as you abandon the river for some time. Bear left to a footbridge on another channel, then out on a grassy path through open pasture. Meeting a fence, the path goes right with it as far as a footbridge. Wooden boards cross an unkempt enclosure to a stile back out, then bear right with a fence to become enclosed past the grounds of a house. A stile in the wall beyond sends a grass track left to join the valley road at Rowleth Wath as it approaches the returning Swale at Rowleth Wood.

Follow the road briefly left until it starts to rise away, and here a path rejoins the wooded riverbank. Things soon open out for a longer spell until a steep, wooded bank forces the path up steps and along to a pair of roadside bridle-gates. Without setting foot on tarmac take the left one into a field, and a concrete track drops steeply away. This super moment reveals the village ahead beyond innumerable parallel walls. An alternative direct finish takes a bee-line through these meadows, a particularly tempting and infallible option in early summer. To enjoy the Swale's company, a thin path bears left to the river, and before the field-end a small gate in the adjacent wall puts you back onto its bank.

A path now follows it back to just short of Gunnerside Beck and Gunnerside New Bridge. Here turn for the village at a gate by a barn, and cross to a stile in the tapering corner. Advance to another into a barnyard, keeping right of the barns to a stile at the end. Through a tiny enclosure a stile puts you into the last field, using a stile at the far left corner to emerge back into the centre alongside the pub.

The Swale below Gunnerside

$4\frac{1}{4}$ miles from Low Row

Low Row's attractive surrounds feature a super combination of riverside and moorland rambling

Start *Village centre (SD 986983; DL11 6PF), roadside parking below pub*
Map *OS Explorer OL30, Yorkshire Dales, North/Central*

Low Row straddles the valley road for a good mile, and incorporates the twin hamlet of Feetham. A long open 'green' runs parallel with the road, focal point being where the church and pub are sited. The imposing Punchbowl Inn dates from 1638, alongside is Holy Trinity church. A quoits pitch sits on the green below the pub. From the pub head west on the grassy bank past the church to cross a side road, before a short green way drops to briefly join the road. Turn right to a Wesleyan church of 1901 and adjacent Literary Institute and Assembly Room of 1909, and here fork right.

As this access road rapidly swings right, advance straight on the left-hand grassy way in front. Keep right at a fork to pass a house, a grassy path continuing to the end house, Brass Napper Hall. Drop away on its access road, but as it doubles sharply back down to the road, take a firm track straight ahead above a wooded bank. After a ford/footbridge it starts to climb away: immediately through a gate go left on a wallside path beneath scrub to quickly emerge onto the base of a colourful sloping pasture. Merging into a broader way, before the end slant left down into trees, dropping to a gate back onto the road by the Crackpot junction. Cross the grassy triangle down onto the side road dropping to Isles Bridge.

Don't cross, but take a small gate on the left to shadow the Swale downstream. Clinging to its bank for a good mile and a half, this super section of riverbank features Low Row across the river. After an early embankment an intriguing wall-top section demands caution, especially if damp. After a wooded bend normal progress resumes, with a lengthy embankment leading into a sheep pasture. Several simple bridges on streamlets feature as the exquisite path crosses a second one. Entering Feetham Wood, the path soon leaves the river, rising through the trees to double back left onto the valley road. Turn briefly right to pass a solitary house at Robin Gate, immediately after which take a stile on the left.

Ascend past the grounds to a gateway behind, then a grassy track climbs very steeply to a gate at the top right corner. Pause to look up-dale to Low Row and beyond, a memorable Swaledale scene (see cover). Advancing to a crumbling wall, the scattered hamlet of Kearton forms a surprisingly populated scene. Bear left towards the house ahead at Park End, and from a stile to its left, ascend near the wall to a stile halfway up. Cross the base of a field to another beneath a cottage at Brockma Gill, with a gate/stile just up behind alongside the house. Ignoring its steep drive, a stile on the left sends a path across a field bottom to a corner gate above the next house. Go right onto its drive, which leads out as a rough road to a gate onto grassy moorland.

This leads out past a house and a mast, rising to a brow and past Gallows Top to the Langthwaite road on Feetham Pasture. Cross straight over along an access track serving two cottages at Bird's Nest. A thin path continues on, quickly reaching a corner of the moor where it becomes enclosed by broadly spaced walls. Dropping pleasantly down to emerge onto the hairpin bend of an access road, turn left to wind steeply back down into Low Row.

Isles Bridge

3¾ miles from Healaugh

A memorable ascent of Swaledale's best known and shapeliest hill

Start Village centre (SE 018990; DL11 6UA), parking area at east end
Map OS Explorer OL30, Yorkshire Dales, North/Central   *Access Open Access, see page 4*

Once the important manor hereabouts, today Healaugh is a sleepy backwater of tidy stone cottages. Turn up the side road past a pair of stone troughs, and at a green bear left on a short access road. Keep left as it runs on by a bungalow, immediately after which take an enclosed grassy path right. Just yards short of the end take a corner stile on the left, and go right along the field edge to another. Now bear right to a stile, then left to one just left of a barn. Joining a driveway, turn right up it to Thiernswood Hall.

The track keeps straight on past the house into trees, now as a path to quickly emerge via a gate at the end. Ascend the small pasture, ignoring a gate ahead in favour of a corner wall-stile just above you. Now in dense bracken in open country, a path runs a few yards to meet a better one from the gate. Rising pleasantly away, it soon escapes the bracken and broadens to rise steadily near the left-hand wall. Through open moorland surrounds it alights onto a rough access road at the lone house of Nova Scotia. Cross straight over onto a better grassy track, soon rising grandly through heather beneath a walled enclosure to merge with another track just beyond. Just yards to the left bear right up a thinner, broad way to the corner of another walled enclosure.

This is the walk's turning point. Taking advantage of Open Access, a thin trod ascends past reeds outside the enclosure. At the top corner head straight up the slope: a faint path might be found but it matters little as you soon reach a clearer, level path beneath a distinct brow. Go left on this a short way to reach a cross-paths on a minor brow, with a grassy knoll just to your left. The already expansive moorland views are joined by the sudden appearance of Arkengarthdale ahead: a super moment. Now turn right on a clear path raking up the flank to pass beneath a cairn and a rash of stones. With Calver Hill's highest reaches just ahead, the path runs a delightful course across a level plateau. When the heather peters out, the path traverses beneath higher ground on your left. A further heather patch precedes a short, steep pull left to a small cairn on the skyline. The substantial summit cairn is now just a couple of minutes further, at around 1598ft/487m.

The summit of Calver Hill is a classic Swaledale viewpoint, with much of the valley on show: the Iron Age earthwork of Maiden Castle is distinct beneath brooding Harkerside Moor opposite, much of Arkengarthdale is seen beneath Fremington Edge, while the valley itself winds up-dale past Low Row. Leave by dropping right, bound for a solitary section of old wall on Riddings Rigg at the foot of the immediate steeper slopes. A faint path drops steeply between scattered stones, improving as it curves down to follow the wall to its far end. Here turn right, a clear path through the heather dropping pleasantly to meet a firm access track at a wall corner. Turn right, soon descending with bird's-eye views of Healaugh. It slants down to a solitary house and then down to Thirns Farm. Here turn left, at once becoming surfaced to drop steeply back into the village.

Healaugh and Calver Hill

4¹4 miles from Grinton

Colourful surrounds and glorious views high above Grinton, with a fine lead mining site

Start Village centre (SE 046984; DL11 6HH), roadside parking
Map OS Explorer OL30, Yorkshire Dales, North/Central

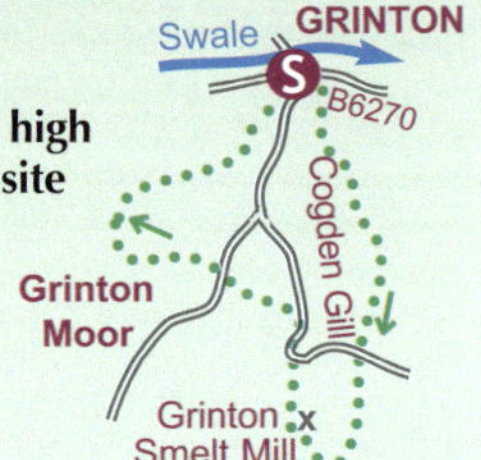

For a note on Grinton see page 34. Leave by the side road climbing past the church, and soon go left over a little footbridge. Pass between houses to a small gate into a field, and cross to a corner stile onto the B6270. Without setting foot on it, take an adjacent stile to ascend a wallside. Through a gate at the top, rise to a stile by a stone shed. Above is Grinton Lodge youth hostel in a 200-year old shooting lodge. Here the path forks: ignore a stile ahead and slant left to one at the top corner, then up to another just ahead. Slant right through two further fields, then across a smaller one to a stile in front of Cogden Gill. Through a bridle-gate ahead slant into the gill, devastated by flash floods in 2019.

A path through bracken up the opposite flank can be hard to locate, so preferably cross the beck immediately on suitable stones and ascend steeply between heather and hawthorns. Quickly easing, continue to the wall just above. Now go right close by it for a briefly unkempt few minutes. The wall drops slightly to a stile at a kink. Views look back to Reeth, Calver Hill, Arkengarthdale and Fremington Edge. Bear right up the large pasture to a gate that soon appears on the skyline. Meeting a grassy track here, pass through to rise across a moor to a wall-gate onto a road.

Cross to a green way rising onto vast Grinton Moor, soon levelling beneath Sharrow Hill's quarried knoll. Just past a triple-arched limekiln is a fork: take that rising gently left to soon meet the line of a flue. This 1080ft tunnel carried fumes from the lead smelting mill below to a moortop chimney. Follow its partially collapsed upper section briefly left up to its abrupt terminus at the chimney site. Now turn right on a slim, level path through heather until you see a rising track to the right. Reaching a reedy ditch, turn down its near side for 50 yards to the track. Double back down its inviting course, merging into another to slant down to 19th century Grinton Smelt Mill with its adjacent peat store. Resume on the main track downstream towards the nearby road. A grassy left fork just before it takes you down to its bridge on the gill. The previous bridge was washed away in the 2019 floods. Across, advance 100 yards to a path slanting left up the moor. After curving in to cross a dry gill, it rises to trace it gently up to a road.

Across, a similar, level grassy way runs through heather with the prow of Harkerside ahead and Reeth across the valley. Meeting a rising grass track by grouse butts, a thin path continues a little further to a shooters' track. Go briefly left, and after a bend left, take a path slanting right down to often-dry Grinton Gill. Doubling back out the other side it runs across the moor, with a fence nearby on the left. Dropping to pass through a fence-gate ahead, it forks: take the main right branch. A super descent to another fence-gate off the moor resumes down grassy slopes with a wall to your left. When the path slants right, take a thinner trod straight down to a small gate by a barn. A faint way descends a large field centre to a corner stile, then down a wallside to a stile in it at a fence. Bear left across a smaller field to a corner gate, where a short enclosed way runs out onto a road, going left to drop back to the start.

Grinton Smelt Mill

4¾ miles from Grinton

Easy walking with valley scenery and distant views on the return

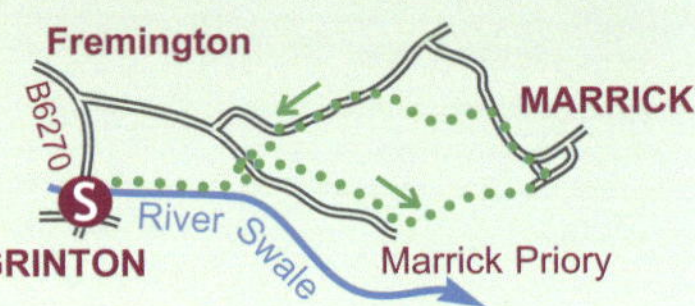

Start Village centre (SE 046984; DL11 6HH), roadside parking
Map OS Explorer OL30, Yorkshire Dales, North/Central

Grinton features the Bridge Inn, St Andrew's church, a Literary Institute of 1903, and WC. Until a chapel was established at Muker in 1580, Grinton parish was one of the largest in the land, extending the full length of the dale to the Westmorland border. Between church and river is Blackburn Hall, a manor house with sections believed to be much older than its 1635 datestone. From the pub cross the bridge and turn right on a path enjoying a good spell by the Swale's wooded bank until emerging into open pasture. Here it bears left up the bank to a gate onto Marrick Priory's access road. From a stile opposite, turn right to rise gently away to a gate/stile above an outer fence corner. Good views look back up-dale, with Harkerside Moor and Calver Hill dominant.

A string of stiles now lead through the fields, on a largely level course aiming for the priory tower, largely with a clear little path. A nice wooded bank rises to the left, while Ellerton Moor fills the skyline ahead. In the last field, slant down to a corner gate/stile back onto the road at the priory entrance. Founded in the early 12th century for Benedictine nuns, the greater part of the remains have been converted into a residential outdoor education centre. Alongside is Priory Farm.

Just after a cattle-grid by the buildings, a gate on the left sends a grassy path slanting up to a bridle-gate into Steps Wood, and a gem of a flagged pathway climbs through it. Known as the Nuns' Causey, it still serves its centuries-old purpose of linking priory with village. On leaving the wood a grassy path remains with the right-hand wall as the going eases, and through gates by a barn it continues as a grassy track to become a surfaced lane on the edge of Marrick. You enter by an old Wesleyan Chapel, with the former St Andrew's mission church of 1858 just beyond. The village stands at a blustery thousand feet up, and this sleepy backwater knew far busier times in the heyday of lead mining. The observant will discover a number of sundials. At the first junction go straight ahead, quickly swinging left to a T-junction in the village centre by a phonebox and nearby Institute. Go left, keeping right to leave the village past Barf House Farm.

Dropping towards a dip, take a stile on the left and follow a wall away. At a stile cross to its other side and remain with it over an early brow. This reveals Calver Hill, while Reeth soon appears beneath it, with Swaledale stretching away to the dalehead skyline and the great sweep of Grinton Moor to the left. This super section drops gently through two intervening gates/stiles to a gate onto the old Richmond road at Reels Head. A steep descent of this quiet lane ensues, quickly passing a well-preserved limekiln. Also well seen during the descent is Grinton, with Grinton Lodge youth hostel high on the moor above. Part way down, beyond a drive to The Hagg on the right, look out for a wall-stile on your left. From here slant right down the large pasture, bearing further right lower down to rejoin your outward route at the stile onto Marrick Priory access road. Cross to retrace steps along the riverbank.

Grinton church

4 miles from Reeth

A pleasant village reached by riverbank, returning on the edge of moorland

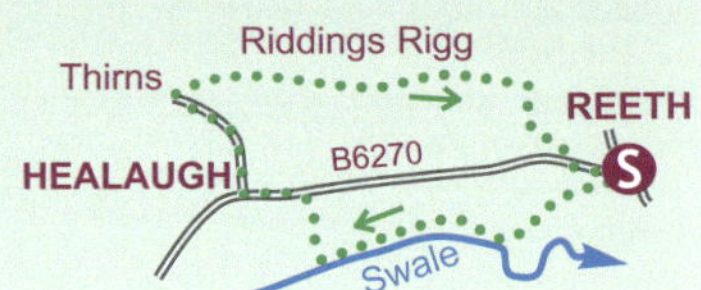

Start *Village centre (SE 038993; DL11 6SW), parking by green*
Map *OS Explorer OL30, Yorkshire Dales, North/Central*

Reeth is the capital of Swaledale within the National Park. It boasts an enviable position on the slopes of Calver Hill, well above the Swale and Arkle Beck confluence. Central is a large, sloping green, with the main buildings stood back on all sides. This old market town exudes a confident air, with inns, shops and tearooms alongside the green with its quoits pitch: there is also an information centre and craft shops. Parking limitations result in an untidy scene around the green in summer, amplified when market traders set up stall on Fridays. Indelibly linked with lead mining days, Reeth has an absorbing folk museum, while annual agricultural shows and festivals add cultural attractions.

From the green pass along the front of the Kings Arms and Black Bull to a contrastingly tiny green at Anvil Square. Across it, to the right, a 'to the river' sign sends a snicket off between walls. Emerging onto a narrow road, advance to join a suburban street. Go left to a junction, then right along a narrow lane to its demise at the last house. A rough lane continues, with a raised, flagged footway alongside. Harkerside Moor dominates across the river. At the end turn left down an enclosed way to emerge at a gate by a barn. Just below, a bridle-gate on the right sends a fenced path between pastures to a suspension footbridge on the River Swale.

Don't cross but turn upstream, a good path clinging tightly to the bank until emerging into open pasture for a delectable section on grassy banks. Becoming part enclosed again, the path runs on to reach stepping-stones on the river. Here leave by a bridle-gate set back on the right and follow the wallside away. Rising to a gate you join the B6270 at a green on the edge of

Healaugh, turning left into the tiny village centre. Turn up the side road past a pair of stone troughs, and passing a green at the top the road climbs out of the village through a gate. It continues more steeply up colourful slopes to end at the farm buildings of Thirns. As it forks into access tracks, take the right-hand one climbing steeply to a cottage before continuing up to find level ground. Calver Hill is immediately above as the track runs across the moor, now with a wall for company. When it turns in to a gate, a more inviting track continues on. Soon rejoined by the wall it runs pleasantly along the moor edge, the heather now gone but the views remaining wide.

Above the farm of Riddings the track drops gently down, with the full length of Fremington Edge ahead. As it bends left, keep straight on an inviting grassy path to a prominent cairn with a wall corner just beyond. Here take a final look back to the shapely crest of Calver Hill. Just beyond is a recess where a gate sends the enclosed path of Skelgate down towards Reeth. Its enchanting start later enters foliage and becomes stonier underfoot. Just yards past a bend at a crossing farm track take a stile by a gate on the right, and slant left through a gateway and down to a stile in the bottom corner behind the village school. Just below it a bridle-gate puts you into a short snicket back onto the B6270 alongside the school. Go left on the footway down into the centre.

The Swale below Healaugh, looking to Harkerside

4¹2 miles from Reeth

A richly varied walk by riverbank and moorland, with outstanding views and an ancient gem

Start *Village centre (SE 038993; DL11 6SW), parking by green*
Map *OS Explorer OL30, Yorkshire Dales, North/Central*

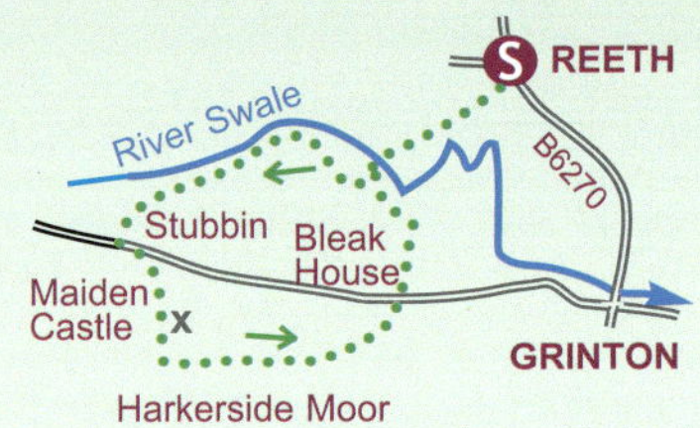

For a note on Reeth see page 36. From the green pass along the front of the Kings Arms and Black Bull to a tiny green at Anvil Square. Across, to the right, a 'to the river' sign sends a snicket off between walls. Emerging onto a narrow road, advance to join a suburban street. Go left to a junction, then right on a narrow lane to its demise at the last house. A rough lane continues, with a raised, flagged footway alongside. Harkerside Moor dominates across the river. At the end turn left down an enclosed way to emerge at a gate by a barn. Just below, a bridle-gate on the right sends a fenced path to a suspension footbridge on the River Swale.

On crossing, note that an informal path turns right to trace the river upstream immediately: the actual right of way heads directly away past a fence corner to join a firm track. Turn right, and just past a section of adjacent wall a bridle-gate in a fence on the right sends a path curving back to the river. Forge on very firmly in nice surroundings to pass stepping-stones opposite Healaugh. A little further is a bridle-gate, then the path slants left up the bank to a wall above. Your lush green way now runs a super level course high above the river, with outstanding views to Healaugh backed by Calver Hill. Remain with the wall until passing through a bridle-gate. Here your path slants left to a gate above. A short-lived path then rises to an unfenced moor road.

Double back left uphill as far as a second bridleway signed right, just as a wall returns after Stubbin Farm. Don't follow it, but take a fine green path directly up into the heather to a skyline tree.

Arrival here is a splendid moment, for Maiden Castle is literally beneath your feet. This ancient earthwork is a defensive site of the Iron Age Brigante tribe: a deep ditch surrounds a tall bank, and the whole is largely unbroken other than its gateway at the far side.

Continue up the path alongside the earthwork, and rising above it is a fork. While the right branch heads for a cairn on a knoll just above, instead rise a few yards further to meet a clear, level path from the cairn. Go left on this along the edge of a modest plateau beneath the steeper flank of Harkerside Moor. This grand stride runs on for some time through the heather, only very gently angling down the moor. Ultimately it arrives at a hard shooters' track in front of a wall. Go briefly left, and at the wall corner just below, escape on an inviting grass track shadowing the wall the short way down to the moor road opposite Bleak House.

There is a good view of Reeth above the lazily winding river, backed by the long skyline of Fremington Edge, while superb examples of strip lynchets (ancient cultivation terraces) fill fields across the river. From a gate left of the house a green way zigzags steeply down to a gate in front of a ruinous farm. To its right, slant right to a wall-stile part way down, then drop to a fence-stile just left of a house. From a small gate behind, descend a large field to a stile just short of the left corner. Joining a firm path, go briefly left to a ditch footbridge, then right with a fence to the suspension bridge to retrace steps.

Maiden Castle, looking to Calver Hill

4^{1}2 miles from Reeth

An airy moorland edge with extensive Arkengarthdale views precedes a valley return

Start Village centre (SE 038993; DL11 6SW), parking by green
Map OS Explorer OL30, Yorkshire Dales, North/Central
Access Open Access, see page 4 (not grouse moors)

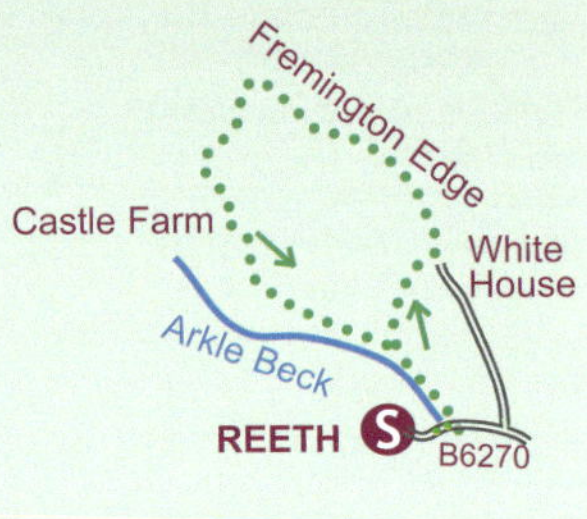

For a note on Reeth, see page 36. Descend the green and follow the Richmond road around to Reeth Bridge on Arkle Beck. Immediately across it, take a stile on the left and go left on a wallside track, with Fremington Edge very dominant high above. When the track leaves, advance to a gate at the end. Cross to the right of a barn ahead, and along to a stile at the end. Now bear right to merge with the right-hand wall, along to a stile in it just above a wooded bank. Leaving the valley floor, cross to a stile opposite then rise on a faint way past a barn to a stile above. You shall return to this crossroads of ways. Now on the steep base of Fremington Edge take the path rising away, bearing slightly left to ascend near an old wall. This proves a pleasant way as it meanders steeply up, partly hollowed, to a brief level halt. Big views look back up-dale to Harkerside Moor and beyond Calver Hill.

Here bear right, slanting up a groove then gently up to the top right corner, where a stile deposits you behind the isolated White House. A grassy way slants up the bracken bank to quickly join a stony old road. Turn left, passing through a gate amid former chert quarries. Steady climbing leads to a guidepost on the crest of Fremington Edge. While the track swings sharp right for the watershed wall, make use of Open Access on an inviting path left on moor grass. From this magnificent stride along the well-defined edge, savour dramatic views across the valley to shapely Calver Hill, with tree-lined Arkle Beck far below.

The path varies in stature but remains clear, rising gently to a cairn amid mining remains then on to the end of a sturdy wall on the edge. A fence-stile sees you resume as far as the second of two further old walls. A cairn just yards before the second of these marks your point of departure, as a path doubles back left. It slants down between rashes of stones to a hollow at the base of the upper edge, then doubles back right on a grassy shelf back towards the old wall. With Castle Farm House directly below, the path drops again, then slanting left down a groove towards the intake wall.

Just short of it, veer left to join and follow it left on a bridleway. Through an old gateway the path continues down above the wall, becoming clearer as a fence takes over: the path runs on down to a gate in a wall ahead. Entering scattered woodland it runs on to merge with a path at an old gateway just above Arkle Beck, at an area devastated by flash floods in 2019. Here take the broad path left, ignoring one dropping to the beck. Ambling through scattered trees you emerge through a gateway amid colourful country, and the broad path forges on with a fading wall. After two further gateways you curve round to the cross-paths on the outward route: through the stile on your right drop down past the barn to return as you came.

Calver Hill from Fremington Edge

4³4 miles from Langthwaite

**A valley walk yet with splendid
views of this relatively little-known dale**

Start *Village centre (NZ 004024;
DL11 6RE), car park on road above*
Map *OS Explorer OL30,
Yorkshire Dales, North/Central*

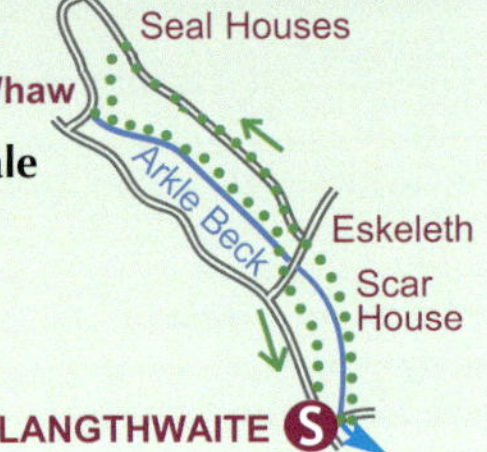

Arkengarthdale is the Swale's major side valley, and Arkle Beck is its fast-flowing, tree-lined tributary. Scattered Langthwaite comprises two distinct sections. Along the through road a range of buildings include St Mary's church of 1819 and the CB (Charles Bathurst) Inn. The other half is clustered below the road on the bank of the beck, centred around the cosy Red Lion with a tiny pinfold opposite. Langthwaite was the centre of the dale's frenzied lead mining industry.

Cross the bridge into the centre, and go left on a short, rough lane before the road climbs steeply away. From a gate at the end a path crosses the field, through a gateway to a stile at the end. The way undulates across two more fields to a large house. At its rear a path slants right up to Scar House, an imposing shooting lodge. Follow the drive briefly down to a sharp bend left, and as the earlier house appears to your left, go a few strides right to locate a path into trees. It runs right on a steep bend above the beck, rising slightly to a footbridge with another just beyond into a field. The faint path curves round above a stone shed to a stile into a large field. Go right by the wall to a stile onto a road at Stang Bridge.

Cross straight over for an appreciable pull up the side road opposite, following this quiet byway for a mile and a third. Opening out into rough pasture at Low Eskeleth, it climbs further then runs on to High Eskeleth before easing out on bracken-clad Low Moor. Through a gate after some seats on a knoll the road leaves the moor, and passes an immense limekiln. Continue along the road past a couple more farms at Seal Houses, and leave by a stile on the left after a gate at a group of modern barns just before a house. From another stile just below, bear slightly left down through two further ones to one into the top of a wooded bank. A little path runs left, then doubles back right down to a pair of stiles out of the trees at the hamlet of Whaw. A path crosses a grassy bank to approach a former Wesleyan chapel of 1840, where double back left to a ladder-stile and out onto the road.

Turn left to the bridge, and without crossing advance to a gate downstream. A faint grass track crosses three fields to approach the beck. At the end of the first is a small preserved cowhouse. A generally thin path continues, briefly by the beck then across a field centre to a wooded corner. Ignoring a footbridge on the beck, continue through a long, open pasture. Back by the tree-lined beck, stiles lead in and out of a wooded corner to emerge by a house. Advance on by the beck through further fields to a footbridge just short of Eskeleth Bridge. Across it turn downstream to a stile onto the road. Before taking the right-hand gate opposite, a short detour up the road reveals, over the wall on the right, a hexagonal powder store from lead mining days. Back at the gate a firm track heads away past a house. Becoming enclosed it swings left towards Old School House: just before it, take a stile on the right and cross to Scar House drive. Follow this right to emerge onto the road at the church. Go left on a footway to finish, passing a former Wesleyan chapel of 1882 and a WC.

Arkle Beck at Eskeleth Bridge

4¹4 miles from Langthwaite

Fine beck, moorland and lead mining scenery in the colourful heart of Arkengarthdale

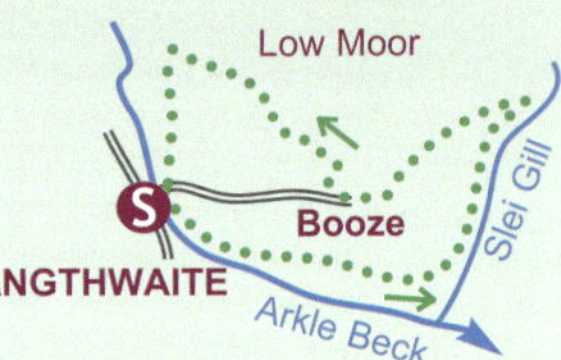

Start Village centre (NZ 004024;
DL11 6RE), car park on road above
Map OS Explorer OL30, Yorkshire Dales, North/Central

For a note on Langthwaite see page 42. Cross the bridge into the heart of the village and turn right behind the first house, opposite the Red Lion. A firm track traces Arkle Beck downstream before striking away into a wood. At a fork take the broader track left, rising to level out before leaving the trees at a gate. The track crosses a field to a gateway, enjoying views ahead to Fell End, with Fremington Edge stretching beyond. While the main track drops to Storthwaite Hall, keep straight on the grassy path ahead into the side valley of Slei Gill. It crosses several enclosures above the gill until a stile heralds arrival at the remains of Tanner Rake Hush Lead Mine. A superb, embanked green way winds between spoilheaps amid Slei Gill's once busy 19th century mining scene.

Beyond the workings a delectable, well-engineered grassy slant leads to an old gateway, just as the gill's confines narrow. Looking back, Calver Hill rises across the main valley. At this point leave by another inviting green way doubling sharply back left immediately before the gateway. It runs a gentle slant looking down on the mining site, through an old wall to an island barn. Passing left of this it undulates through further mining remains and rises very gently out of the site to an outer wall corner just ahead. Here a farm track leads along the wallside to a gate, and on again to one behind a barn, where it becomes briefly enclosed to reach Town Farm at Booze. This jovially named little settlement perches on a green patchwork hillside, its only link with the outside world being the lane from Langthwaite. At the other end follow the concrete access road up through the hamlet.

Levelling out, it runs on with a parallel drive above. After this joins, continue a little further until another drive doubles sharply back uphill. Reaching a gate to Fountain House Farm, instead slant back left up an inviting path above a ruin. Becoming sunken, it rises between old walls to a bridle-gate. It continues rising, curving right more steeply to a gate above. Rise through a few reeds with a wall to your right, quickly joining a grassy track coming out from a gate. This climbs to a gate in a wall at the top.

Entering heathery Low Moor, the gently rising track quickly merges into a harder one from the right. Rising imperceptibly, advance on for a third of a mile until approaching a steeper little rise on a bend right. With a grassy knoll on your right, turn off left the short way to the nearby wall, locating a bridle-gate in a recess. Entering more remains, a grassy path drops away alongside an old wall amid rugged surrounds where old shafts lurk. Leaving the old wall lower down, it drops into more open country, now as a broad green way past scattered rocks to a gateway in the wall below. Through it turn left on a grassy path between wall and steep woodland, passing beneath the long derelict Scar Top House. Quickly approaching the trees ahead, it begins a slant down, through a bridle-gate into the trees. This super path enjoys a non-claustrophobic, gentle slant down to the wood bottom. Here it goes left with the wall to emerge onto the steep Booze lane just above the roofs of Langthwaite.

The Red Lion Inn, Langthwaite

4¹4 miles from Hurst

An upland stroll with airy views sandwiched between extensive lead mining remains

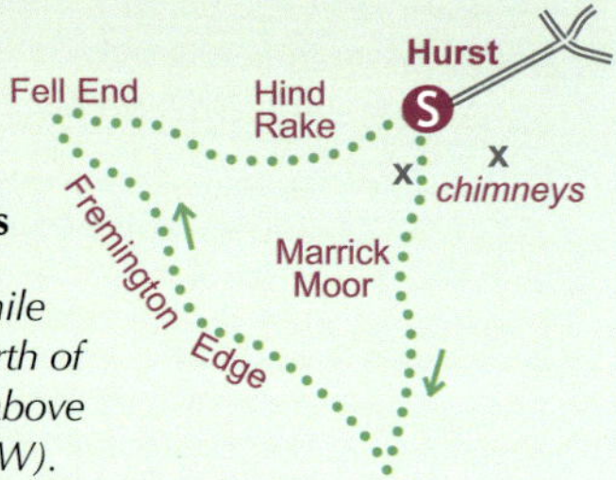

Start Surfaced road-end half-mile west of phonebox 2¹2 miles north of Fremington-Marske crossroads above Marrick (NZ 046023; DL11 7NW).
Tidy fenceside verge parking opposite last house
Map OS Explorer OL30, Yorkshire Dales, North/Central

Hurst is a very remote, tiny community amid profuse lead mining remains, though it is difficult now to imagine it in its 19th century industrial peak. The Green Dragon Inn only closed its doors in the late 1970s, while the old school building also survives. Just yards back along the road, a gate on the right sends a firm track up into sprawling mining environs. Almost at once on your right is a well-preserved four-square chimney, with another set back over to the left. Quickly reaching a fork, stay on the main track through a gate ahead. Head away at a much gentler gradient across heathery Marrick Moor, with vast mine debris to the right.

With sections of excellent grass verges, the track rises ever gently into heather and the wall parts company. Reaching a brow Swaledale's moorland skyline is revealed, and the track drops gently to a gate in a sturdy wall ahead. Advancing just a few yards reveals a near bird's-eye prospect of Reeth in its enviable setting. Whilst the very rough track immediately briefly forks, instead opt for a grassy path just to its right, which makes a short drop to a seat alongside a level path on the crest of Fremington Edge. Making use of Open Access this inviting path rises right on moor-grass to enjoy a magnificent stride along the edge. This will remain your course for a mile and three-quarters' march to Fell End. Fully savour the dramatic views over Arkengarthdale: across the valley is shapely Calver Hill, with tree-lined Arkle Beck far below.

The path varies in stature but remains clear throughout, rising gently to a substantial cairn amid mining remains, then on to the end of a sturdy wall on the edge. A fence-stile sees you resume, with the second of two further crumbled walls featuring a parallel fence-stile preceded by a cairn. Beyond another crumbled wall you curve around the edge's highest section to a cairn at around 1540ft/470m. A more pronounced drop now works its way around the curving edge. Through more old workings the path drops to adjacent fence and ladder-stiles, then crosses a broad grassy way and through a minor dip before the slightest of rises to a graceful cairn on Fell End. Be aware that steep, craggy ground drops away beneath the cairn to the extensive remains of Fell End Lead Mine. Ahead beyond intervening Slei Gill are the hamlet of Booze and Booze Moor's heathery expanses.

From this turning point ignore a clear path right, and instead double back sharply right on a thinner but clear path, crossing easy ground towards a prominent cairn. Here you meet a broader green bridleway on the edge of the mining area, its two similar strands rapidly merging. Bear right, passing beneath spoilheaps to rise very gently to a gate at a wall junction. Back on the heather moor, take the main path rising left to quickly meet a firm, level track. Leaving the Arkengarthdale scene go right on this, soon entering another extensive mining scene as it slants right to make a very steady descent of Hind Rake, with Hurst Dam well seen down to the left. At the bottom drop to a gate off the moor, with the starting point just in front.

Smelt mill chimney, Hurst

4¹4 miles from Hurst

A fascinating ramble around a secret lead mining valley in an unsung corner

__Start__ Hamlet centre (NZ 052025; DL11 7NW), small parking area by phonebox at crossroads 2¹2 miles north of Fremington-Marrick crossroads above Marrick.
__Map__ OS Explorer OL30, Yorkshire Dales, North/Central

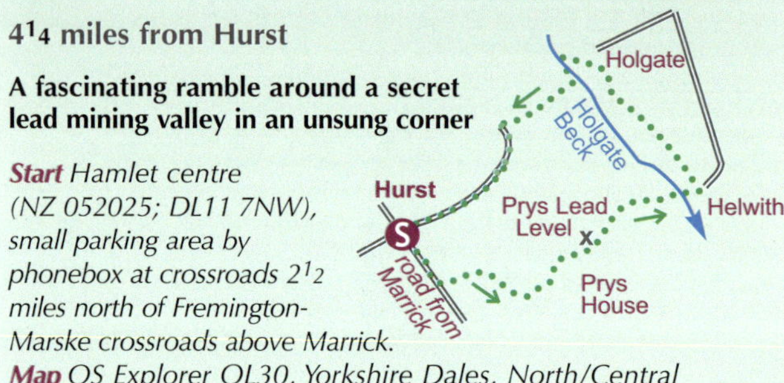

For a note on Hurst see page 46. From the junction head back up the road you arrived on, a steady pull with the mining site of Queen's Lead Level on your right. Just short of the brow go left on Prys House Farm access road, which drops gently away. After a cattle-grid it slants across a field centre to another grid, then down an extensive pasture to the site of Prys Lead Mine at the bottom. Just before starting to climb away, instead bear left on a level grassy way, passing a clump of trees and dropping alongside a hollow to a corner gate. Take the path bearing right, dropping again with the ditch to a secretive corner where you pass through a gate beneath a craggy bluff. The path swings round a corner to emerge, passing beneath further crags in a delightful drop towards Prys Lead Level, with the sizeable ruin of a mine shop alongside the slabby bed of Shaw Beck.

A little past a trench, cross a stone-arched bridge on the stream. The path resumes along the other bank past the substantial chambers of a bouseteam (ore store) and varied other remains. Beyond the site the path runs through bracken above the beck, through an old gateway and out through a flat rabbit warren to reach a confluence with Holgate Beck. Cross your stream to a gate onto a stony track dropping through a gate to a ford/footbridge on the main beck. Across, a short walled way enters the hamlet of Helwith, with its seasonal tea garden.

Take the narrow access road climbing left only as far as a hairpin bend, and take a slim stile on the left. A little path heads away, rising to a bridle-gate beneath a house. Rising slightly by its fence it crosses a large sloping field, then fades as you rise more to a stile in the wall ahead. Now largely pathless, forge on across a string of parallel walls, with stiles later replaced by gateways. As the derelict yet once substantial farm of Holgate appears ahead, a grassy way runs to it. Advance into the unkempt yard amid a scene of haunting decay. With the old house in front, drop left to a gateway in the wall dropping away.

Head across a sloping field, dropping left across a little bank to a gateway in a wall, with a fence ahead. Entering bracken a path drops right, parallel with an old wall. Briefly fading, drop through a few yards of dense bracken to meet another path. Go right, slightly uphill, to run through further bracken to a bridle-gate onto a stony track. Drop to Goats Bridge footbridge/ford on Holgate Beck, and climb the steep, stony track away. It soon levels out for a brief walled section to a gate, then on a fieldside to a gate onto open moor. Head away to a junction, turning left to immediately become surfaced with good verges. Rising to a brow, it runs to a cattle-grid off the moor. Enclosed by walls it quickly drops away to return you to the start, the final short section being slightly uphill.

The ford at Helwith

3^{1}2 miles from Marske

Splendid varied surroundings in a little-known valley, featuring quality woodland and moorland

Start *Village centre (NZ 104004; DL11 7LU), parking by bridge (honesty box)*
Map *OS Explorer OL30, Yorkshire Dales, North/Central **or** 304, Darlington & Richmond*
Access *Open Access, see page 4 (not grouse moor)*

Marske is a delightful place on the National Park boundary, with mellow cottages amongst colourful gardens and embowered in noble trees. Hidden away is the large hall, now apartments. Above the old bridge is the church of St Edmund, featuring much Norman work. Astride the old Richmond to Reeth road, today Marske is known more to slower paced travellers on the Coast to Coast Walk: the church even operates a tuck shop. Climb from the bridge to a junction above the church, and turn left. When it rapidly turns uphill, remain on the level cul-de-sac. Note a much older sundial on the building of 1907 by an old North Riding roadsign.

At the last house (the former school), the road loses its surface as it opens out into a field. Passing the hamlet of Clints, note the curiously-shaped former Methodist chapel. A broad carriageway forges on through the sylvan paradise of Clints Wood. Part way up a gentle but sustained rise, bear left on a broad, level path to quickly leave the trees at a gate to emerge into open pasture. On the skyline high above are the limestone cliffs of Clints Scar. The superb green way meanders along to approach the house at Orgate Farm. Just before it, turn down the access road to cross Marske Beck by footbridge or ford. Orgate Force is visible just upstream, but the path up the bank is not a right of way.

The access road climbs to a junction by a barn, where turn right on the drive to Telfit Farm. This quickly passes through a gate to lose its tarmac in open country beneath Telfit Bank. Only a short way along, after a small barn and as far as a gate on the right where the first field ends, make brief use of Open Access by taking a grass track slanting left into bracken. It quickly becomes clearer as it rises alongside its original sunken way. Soon turning sharply to slant left, a steady rise leaves the bracken and eases out on approaching a stony track and wall at the top of the bank. Delightful views look over this charming side valley. Turn left on this track through a gate in a wall for a gentle descent above the bank, and at the next gate it become enclosed to drop more steeply and stonily down onto the valley road.

Turn briefly right to a stile on the left by a stone shed. A grassy path crosses the field diagonally to a kissing-gate beneath a row of trees, then follow a fence away. When it turns left beyond an intervening bridle-gate, go straight on to drop to the substantial stone-arched Pillimire Bridge. Enveloped in foliage just before it is the surprising sight of an old waterwheel. Across the bridge a little path turns right, along the foot of a bank to meet the beck again. Here it encounters a potentially muddy section before a bridle-gate into trees. The beckside path rapidly reaches a flight of stone steps up onto Marske Bridge to finish.

The Marske Valley under Orgate Scar

4¹2 miles from Richmond

Fine woodland and riverbank on the edge of a famous town

Start Town centre (NZ 171008; DL10 4QN), car parks
Map OS Explorer 304, Darlington & Richmond

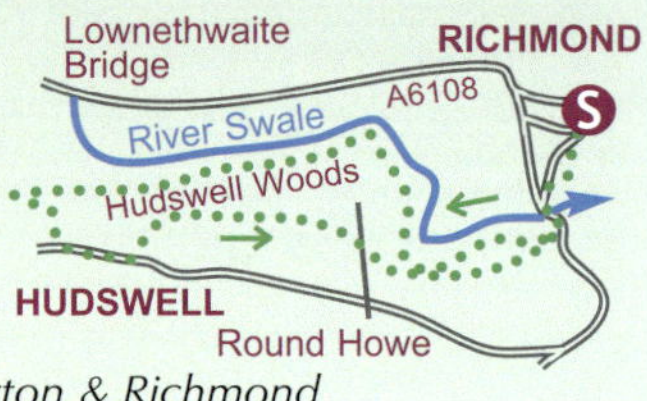

For a note on Richmond, see page 54. From the south-west corner of Market Place descend New Road, within yards bearing left on a cobbled way (The Bar) that drops beneath an arch (part of 14th century town walls) onto Bridge Street. Go left to The Green, and keep left to cross the Swale on Richmond (Green) Bridge, with a classic castle view. Across, take a broad path upstream into trees. At an early fork keep left, a broad path slanting up Billy Bank Wood. Beneath a quarried face and a long line of smaller crags, you reach a junction at a bend looking down on a river bend. Keep straight on, soon slanting gently down to a kissing-gate into a pasture. Cross to a riverside path and go left on a broad green way, becoming firmer as wooded slopes close in to reach a footbridge on the Swale to Round Howe car park/WC.

Ignoring the bridge and any other paths, resume upstream through Hudswell Woods, down a few early steps to regain the bank. An encounter with a sandy beach precedes a super section with the river. Past an old quarry a fork is reached: take the left one, slanting gently to mid-height and passing beneath substantial cliffs. Further, at a fork, ignore the right branch dropping to the river and go a little further to Hudswell Steps. Cross straight over to a small gate out of the wood. A path heads away, slanting gently on across scrubby slopes. At a junction with a path slanting down from the left, double back left up its pleasant course to meet a higher path. At a cross-paths with Hudswell Steps just ahead, climb the 32 steps into a field, and a path ascends to a small gate at the top. This sends an enclosed path to the road in Hudswell, where go left past the George & Dragon pub.

A little beyond the village hall take a gap on the left to a gate into a field, and descend to a corner one. A path drops through scrub into a clearing, and forks. Back in the wood top, take the right-hand path dropping briefly through scrub onto a level wood-top path. Turn right to cross a mini ravine for a largely level stroll above steep wooded slopes. Soon you ascend 13 wooden steps to resume along a field outside the wood. Go left through a bridle-gate to another back into trees. Resume as before, soon reaching a fork. This time take the small gate out into open pasture.

Angle away to a bridle-gate in a hedge, then on with the hedge to one at the end. Cross an open area to another into trees, soon reaching a stile back out and across a field corner to a hedge-stile. A very brief enclosed section leads to a stile into a field, and along to another in a hedge ahead. Cross to one ahead and resume to a bridle-gate back into trees, with a little gate rapidly back out. Curve round the wood edge a little further, but before the corner bear right to a hedge-stile ahead. Bear right to another, then cross between slim enclosures before slanting slightly right through two further stiles to one into a large equestrian pasture. Bear very slightly right to a dip where the wood comes up. Over a stile a path runs to one back into trees: ignore it and keep on the grass path above the wood to a corner kissing-gate. A firm path enters trees, and the river re-appears beneath an exceedingly steep drop. The path runs along the top before slanting down a part sunken way. It emerges onto the road on the other side of the house where you left it by the bridge: now retrace opening steps. *Richmond Castle*

**3³4 miles
from Richmond**

**A stroll to a magnificent
monastic ruin by the Swale**

*Start Town centre (NZ 171008;
DL10 4QN), car parks
Map OS Explorer 304 - Darlington & Richmond*

Richmond is the gateway to Swaledale, steeped in history and dominated by the castle on its promontory above the Swale: its enormous 12th century keep watches over the whole town. Lined by shops, pubs and cafes, the vast Market Place has in the centre of its sloping cobbles Holy Trinity church with a 14th century tower: it incorporates the Green Howards Museum. Outside of the square from which numerous wynds (narrow ways) radiate is St Mary's church with a 14th century tower. Grey Friars Tower stands across from the Georgian Theatre of 1788, while Culloden Tower is near the river, which flows between two graceful bridges.

From the south-west corner of Market Place descend New Road, rapidly bearing left on a cobbled way (The Bar) that drops beneath an arch (part of 14th century town walls) onto Bridge Street. Go left to a junction at The Green, noting on the corner a pair of 1720/21 sundials. Go left over the Swale on Richmond (Green) Bridge, with its classic castle view, then turn left to a gate into the football club at Earl's Orchard. A path passes left of the clubhouse to run by the river to reach a fork: take the main one rising to a kissing-gate into South Bank Fields. Take the concession path left, outside trees and opening out along the base of the wildflower meadows to a gate. With fine views to the castle, it continues through two further meadows to Station Bridge (now Mercury Bridge), built to connect the town to its railway station.

Pass under to ascend steps to the bridge alongside the Old Station with its various attractions. This was the final mile of the Richmond branch line that opened in 1846 and closed in 1969. Entering the car park, advance to the far end to gain the terminus of the old line. Now simply head away along the firm pathway, which runs a largely tree-lined course to bridge the Swale, a super vantage point. Across, double back left on a driveway, shadowing the river to the hamlet of Easby, dominated by its magnificent abbey ruins. The Premonstratensian abbey was founded in 1152 by Roald, Constable of Richmond Castle. In its shadow, St Agatha's church dates from the 12th century, and features 13th century wall paintings discovered during Victorian restoration work.

Resume on the short driveway left of the abbey, passing the entrance to end at a house. An enclosed path to its left quickly emerges into a field: go left to a kissing-gate into riverbank trees. Within yards the path forks, take that down steps to the river and follow it upstream amid nice surrounds. At the end it joins a rough access road alongside the Drummer Boy's Stone, a plaque telling its legend. Go left on the road, rising above the river and on to emerge onto Lombards Wynd back in town. Go left the few strides to the A6136, crossing to a surfaced path into the grassy spaces of The Batts. Head away close by the river, and when the main path slants uphill, take one running left to Richmond Falls. Leave through the adjacent car park/WC and up the road to the right, climbing back into town with the keep beckoning. Part way up, double back left along the front of Castle Terrace, and a surfaced path swings round to Castle Walk, a splendid terrace with great river views from the base of the castle walls. At the end it curves around to re-enter the centre where you left it.

Easby Abbey

4 miles from Scorton

Easy strolling to an old church between restored nature reserve lakes

Start Scorton Lakes (NZ 242996; DL10 6AB), easily missed car park on B6271, ³4-mile west of village
Map OS Explorer 304 - Darlington & Richmond

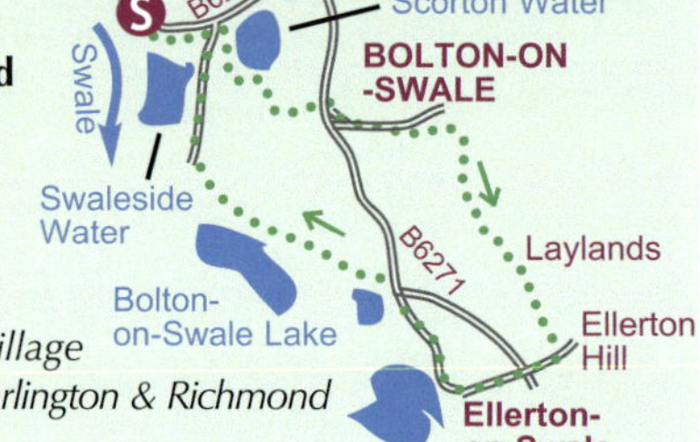

Nearby Scorton is an attractive village sat back from a vast green which doubles as an enormous roundabout. It has a Post office/shop, the Farmers Arms and Heifer pubs, and a Methodist Church of 1909. Prominent at the north-east corner of the green is the distinguished frontage of a grammar school, founded around 1760 but now converted to residential use. Over the road was the Hospital of St John of God: with a Roman Catholic chapel of 1823, it cared for the elderly for over 100 years until the turn of this century. The area south and west of Scorton was extensively quarried for sand and gravel, and since 2008 has been subject to an ongoing transformation into an extensive nature reserve landscape. Several lakes and numerous walking routes have been created, indeed the start point overlooks Swaleside Water.

By information panels a bridle-gate sends an enclosed path east parallel with the road, maintaining this course to meet Back Lane as it leaves the main road. Cross to a bridle-gate sending a path down to another gate on the edge of Scorton Water. Take the path running right outside its boundary fence, at the end swinging left to run above the lake's far side. At the end the path swings right to rise briefly to a bridle-gate onto the enclosed cart track of Flat Lane. Go left, later becoming concrete to emerge back onto the B6271 at Bolton-on-Swale. Cross to the footway and go briefly right to the preserved village pump, then fork left to the church.

This hamlet is known for its churchyard memorial to Henry Jenkins, reputedly born in 1500, and passing on 169 years later. Until recently an inn at Kirkby Malzeard, near Masham, recalled his 'achievement' by name. St Mary's 14th century church has a 16th century tower and refreshments with a donations box. From the church go briefly left on the road, and at a kissing-gate on the right bear left across lush pasture, loosely accompanying Bolton Beck. From a kissing-gate the path traces an arable field edge with little sign of the stream. Through another bridle-gate, part way along the next field, take an easily missed little bridge to resume on the other bank. Quickly emerging from an arable field, a pleasant pasture leads to a bridle-gate onto Laylands farm drive. From one opposite, bear right to a gate behind it for the path to run an enclosed course with the elusive stream to emerge onto a road near Ellerton Hill.

Turn right the short way to a crossroads with the B6271 again at Ellerton Cross, and go straight over on quiet Sled Lane. Ellerton-on-Swale is rapidly reached at a junction. Its scattered houses play support to a country park with café and farm shop. Remain on the road swinging right, its hedgerowed course leading to the B6271 (again!) at Bolton Cross. Don't join but bear left on an enclosed cart track - Back Lane again. This accesses Yorkshire Wildlife Trust's Bolton-on-Swale nature reserve, another revival of old workings hosting a wide range of wildfowl and waders. The lane's pleasant course passes a car park on the right, with access to Bolton-on-Swale Lake on the left inviting a variant finish, featuring bird-hides but with no dogs allowed. The lane becomes surfaced before ignoring Flat Lane to the right. Advance straight on to rejoin your outward route alongside the road, turning left to retrace steps back to the start.

Jenkins Memorial,
Bolton-on-Swale

4³4 miles from Aldbrough St John

The ramparts of an Iron Age fort spread between interesting hamlets

Start Village centre (NZ 202114; DL11 7SZ), roadside parking
Map OS Explorer 304 - Darlington & Richmond

Aldbrough St John is an elegant village set back from greens, with extensive Low Green overlooked by Aldbrough Hall. By High Green are a former Methodist Chapel, pinfold and the Stanwick Arms. From here cross to a packhorse bridge on Aldbrough Beck onto a small green. Go right to distinctive gateposts, through which take a gate on the right and head along a field near the beck. At the tapering end cross a footbridge on inflowing Mary Wild Beck, and through a gate into a rolling pasture. Rise steadily left on a tractor track, crossing the fence on your left at a stile/gate, and resuming with the fence. When it bends gently right to a corner, continue straight up a faint path to a stile/gate ahead. Advancing to a brow, bear gently right down towards a fence where it meets a road. Note the first sighting of Stanwick Fortifications to the left.

From a stile onto the road, go briefly left to one opposite, and head away on a narrow strip by Mary Wild Beck. Through a gate at the end, advance on a streamside path, crossing it towards the end to a stile up onto a road at Kirkbridge by Kirkbridge House. Ignoring the church for now, a bridle-gate opposite sends a grassy path rising away, with a deer shelter to your right at the centre of the 2000-year old Iron Age site. Stanwick Fortifications are a remarkable earthwork of the Brigantes, whose settlement of some 700 acres was defended by a vast network of banks and ditches.

In the top corner a gate sends a short-lived way between wall and wood into a field corner. Go left on a track to a junction on a gentle brow. Turning right, a better track rises gently along a crest between arable fields, then on as a path to shadow Hillhouse

Plantation to a road junction. Turn right on the B6274 down into the hamlet of Forcett. Approaching it, note a distinct section of earthwork to your right. On the left is St Cuthbert's church, just past which are the 18th century gates and lodges of Forcett Hall.

At the junction turn right to another, then right again at an old roadsign. 50 yards further is an information panel, where a kissing-gate puts you up onto the embankment for a short stroll along a fine section. Early steps drop into the ditch to double back to the road. Continue a short way to a rough access road on the right. While the true right of way leaves the road further on, its non-existent access point would force you to tramp across a pathless arable field centre. So common sense sends you right by this track, rapidly leaving it to remain on the fieldside to your left, with a hedge on your right. Advance all the way along to a bridle-gate at the far end. Entering a nicer pasture, bear left for Stanwick church. Moist ground midway may require a detour right towards a stream before returning to a ladder-stile in the churchyard wall.

The church of St John the Baptist features a solid tower dating from the 13th century, while inside are a Viking cross and splendid effigies of Sir Hugh Smithson and his wife. From the porch bear right on the path to a lych-gate onto the road. Turn right to finally cross Kirk Bridge, and remain on the road rising by the earthwork to end at the hamlet of Stanwick St John. As the tarmac ends pass through a gateway left of the final house, swinging right to fork within 50 yards: eschew the continuing track for the fenced path left, running to a gate at a house: note the distinctive earthwork on your left. Keep straight on the driveway to join a road, bearing right to finish.

Stanwick Fortifications

4 miles from Gilling West

Much of interest in and around the quiet valley of Hartforth Beck

Start Village centre (NZ 182050; DL10 5JG), roadside parking
Map OS Explorer 304 - Darlington & Richmond

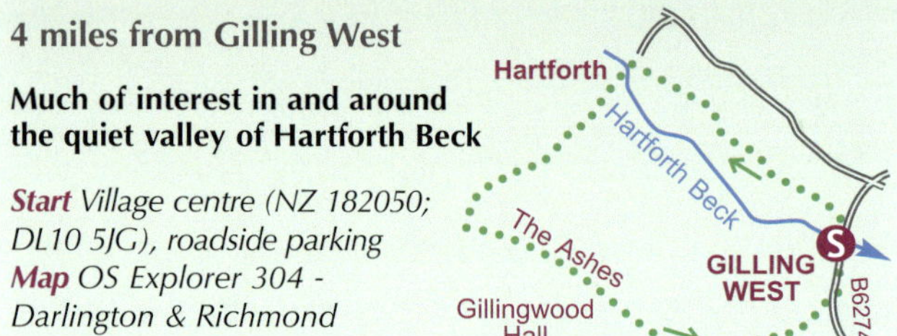

Gilling West is an attractive street village with a green at its northern end. St Agatha's church dates from the 11th century, while the White Swan was a coaching inn. Just along the street is the Angel Inn, also a blacksmith, a florist and a former school of 1847. From the northern end of Gilling Bridge on Gilling Beck, advance just a few strides to a kissing-gate on the left. An enclosed path heads out of the village, and on emerging into a field, runs on to cross an access road. From a bridle-gate behind, commence a super course through numerous pastures. Ultimately entering an arable field, the path surmounts a modest brow and runs arrow-like to the far end to enter the hamlet of Hartforth.

Advance along the short access road to a sharp bend right, then keep on a short way to go left beyond Home Farm. The grassy bridleway of historic Jagger Lane drops to a splendid three-arched bridge on Hartforth Beck. Back to your left is the award-winning 21st century replacement for Home Farm, while upstream is Hartforth Hall, a fine country house of 1744. Across the bridge a trod heads directly away, bearing slightly right to a wooden bridge on a stream. A trod rises away by a line of trees, passing through a broad gap in them with a tree-shrouded pond to your left. The old way becomes sunken and much clearer to pass through a belt of trees. From a bridle-gate it rises right to quickly join a hard track from Crabtree House Farm to the left. Continue up this, ignoring a right branch at a junction where a wall forms on your left. Advance straight on up, passing an old quarry as it levels out.

Through a cattle-grid/gate in front, the track continues up the wallside. As the wall turn sharp left rise slightly further to a gate in the continuing fence, and a grassy way heads off left beneath gorse and trees above the wall. At a gate at the end into a sloping pasture, the path fades but simply trace the wall. At the end bear right on a path outside The Ashes (a wood) up to a gate. Resume on a final fieldside to a gate into Gillingwood Hall's farm environs. A grassy way drops below barns to a gate into the yard, leaving by the access road. To the right are two follies created by the Whartons who occupied the original house destroyed by fire in 1750.

Further on, your way turns sharp left to drop away. Easiest option is to remain on this onto Waters Lane, going right to finish. Otherwise, leave at an early wall-gap on the right, and a thin path drops slightly away across an arable field. At the far side drop left with a fence beneath a wooded bank, soon reaching a gap with a stile just behind. Drop left down a nicer pasture, bearing left to a grassy bridge on a dyke. Bear right to a stile ahead, and on through unkempt surrounds with a wildfowl pond to your right. Soon emerging at the base of a sloping field on your left, cross to a stile a short way up the facing hedge. From another ahead, bear left over the brow to reveal the village ahead. Drop to a corner gate, then along a hedgeside as far as a slim gate/stile by an outbuilding on the right. This sends an enclosed path between gardens to emerge back onto the street. Go left past an old milestone to finish.

Hartforth Beck and Hall

4³⁄4 miles from Ravensworth

A nice range of paths linking characterful hillside villages

Start Village centre
(NZ 140078; DL11 7ET),
roadside parking
Map OS Explorer 304 -
Darlington & Richmond

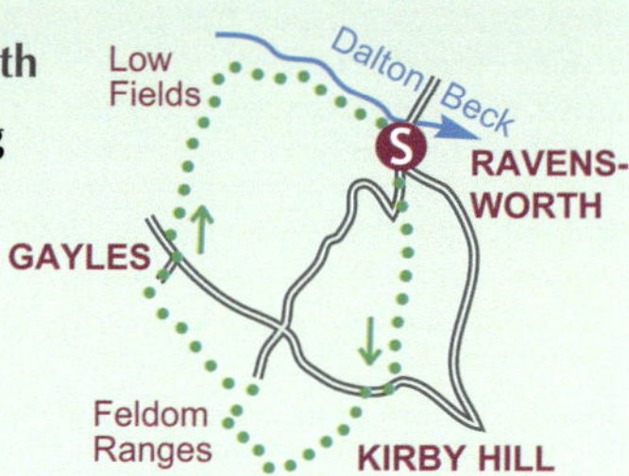

Attractive Ravensworth spreads around extensive greens, while on the village edge are the remains of Ravensworth Castle, a 14th century fortified manor house. Facing the Bay Horse pub, leave by the side road going left across a green to quickly leave past the school. The castle is best seen from this vicinity, across a wildlife pond. As the road quickly bends sharp right, advance straight on over a cattle-grid on Larklands Farm drive. Before long take a stile on the left, over stepping-stones on a streamlet. Slant up the field, crossing a bank and ditch to a stile above. Head away with a wallside path, rising then running to a wall-stile at the end. An initially thin path ascends Saltern Bank, passing a memorial and curving more clearly left to a wall-stile at the top. A little path bears right up a small enclosure to a stile onto a road at Kirby Hill, emerging between the church and the Shoulder of Mutton pub. This tiny village is based around a green dominated by the medieval church of St Peter & St Felix. Around the green are an old grammar school and former almshouses.

Turn right on the road out, but soon leave by an enclosed cart track on the left. Through a gate it passes a double limekiln, and from a gate just behind, slants right up a field centre. Through a facing gate just short of the top corner, the green way of Hergill Lane rises very steadily to meet a firmer access road at the top. To the left and ahead is the MOD's Feldom Ranges. Turn right for a good stride, soon dropping past a lone house to a sharp right turn. Dropping more firmly, leave by a stile/gate set back on the left before reaching Quarry House. A grassy track heads away on a largely level course through the gorse- and bracken-draped environs of the long-abandoned Gayles Quarry.

Emerging, the way fades as you advance with a fence to your right. Crossing a streamlet below a small ravine, cross to a ladder-stile in the wall ahead into Park Wood. Advance a few strides to join a clearer path dropping right, and along to a stile out of the trees. A splendid green way slants down across a pasture to a fence, then dropping briefly to a gate where fence and wall meet. Head away with a fence on your left to a gate onto the access road of Gayles Hall, to your left. Turn down this into the village of Gayles, passing the attractive late 17th century Manor House.

At the through road go briefly left to a shelter, where turn right down the hedgerowed track of Long Lane. On levelling out it runs partly open to the house at Low Fields Barn. Pass to its right, then left between garden and barn into an arable field. Turn right past the barn into the open field, just 50 yards as far as a cross-paths. Turning right, the path runs to a gate in a wall ahead. Cross a smaller field to a colourful knoll, which a small path surmounts. Down the other side to a small gate, bear left to a grassy bank fronting an unused ford on Dalton Beck. Go right on an embankment path that shadows the stream to a stile into a lush pasture. The final stage is a delectable streamside stroll to a gate by an unused arched bridge at the end. A track heads away, swinging right out onto a road in the village, where go right to finish.

Ravensworth Castle

4$\frac{1}{4}$ miles from Surrender Bridge

Heather moorland tracks around an iconic lead mining landmark

Start *Surrender Bridge (SD 988998; DL11 6PP), parking area at moorland junction a mile north of Low Row* **Map** *OS Explorer OL30, Yorkshire Dales, North/Central* **Access** *Open Access, see page 4 (short section only)*

Descend to cross the bridge, and as the road climbs away take a firm track left. Running above Old Gang Beck, it gains only a little height as it runs for about a mile to Old Gang Smelt Mill. The best known and most evocative of Swaledale's 19th century lead mining sites is dominated by a tall chimney. On the hillside above, just beyond, are the remains of the peat store. Beyond the main workings you pass an arched level and restored stone sheds, with a stone-arched bridge on the beck. Remain on the track climbing away, quickly levelling to reach a fork. Here bear left on a level track to cross Level House Bridge on an embankment.

Through a gate behind, the track rises past a mining ruin and another level to quickly reach a junction. Take the more inviting left branch, initially level with a grass strip before a steady rise. Level again for some time, big views open out down the valley between Calver Hill and Harkerside Moor. Another steady rise leads to the high point at 1548ft/472m on Brownsey Moor. Ignoring the main track climbing right, yours starts to drop away, with a wall coming in close to the left. A little further it transforms into a super green way, paralleling the wall down to a gate in a wall off the moor. The even grassier continuation drops towards an outer wall corner, with a firmer track coming up from the hamlet of Blades. Turn left on its initially grassy wallside continuation, rising gently to a gate in a descending wall. Through this enjoy a super, virtually level stride across the open moor of Feetham Pasture to join the road just short of its crest. Go left to drop back to the start.